This book is dedicated to all victims of domestic abuse.

No matter your age, gender, colour or culture, abuse is abuse and we should unite against it, with open minds.

Based on a true story.

Introduction

Murder can happen in many ways. Most domestic violence headlines are direct, brutal murders – invariably by male abusers. What about other methods? The ones that drive victims to suicide or, for example, through extreme sleep deprivation cause a fatal accident? All kill the victim. Media coverage and outrage over these? Doesn't seem to exist.

Does your partner shout at you? Put you down? Accuse you of cheating? Threaten to hurt you or others? Hit you? Control your finances? Tell you who you can meet or where you can go? Be horrible then become nice, then become horrible again in a repeating cycle? If your answer to any of the above is 'yes', you are a victim of domestic abuse, regardless of your gender.

My name is Brad - a therapist specialising in healing domestic abuse and childhood wounds. What follows is the documented true story of domestic abuse and the two children involved. As it unfolds, with thoughts from the victim and transcripts of the actual abuse as it took place, I explore it from a psychological point of view.

Names have been changed – with the couple in question denoted as Victim and Abuser - for this is a story of abuse, not gender. Originally written in 2018, only now the children are adults can this story be fully told - with photographs of those involved.

As in so many cases, there comes the question of why stay? This is something I hope you will come to understand as the complexities and manipulations, of officials as well as the victim, unfold. The abuser's voice is heard through the recordings of attacks, emails, text messages and official logs, including from the police.

Due to a further breach of the indefinite Restraining Order against them, their abuser fled the UK in 2015 to avoid prison but still keeps in touch, via abusive emails from afar - still blaming the victim for everything. Still claiming total innocence, despite the convictions and mass of evidence against them, such as one, 8 months before their removal:

Transcript: 3rd July 2012, 8.15pm

VICTIM	So you're not letting me sleep at all before a 30-hour shift?
ABUSER	Don't care.
VICTIM	So what should I do? Quit?
ABUSER	I want you to die.

You can hear the recording for this, and the other transcriptions in this book on Victim's Youtube channel – details in Conclusions. XXXX is used when the recorded words are unclear or an identifying detail/name has been redacted.

All photographs, videos, transcripts, police logs, emails, texts and social service reports are real - from the actual events as they unfolded.

Victim's words are included in dark blue, as below:

"I'm not doing this book just to empower others to escape. It's also about showing the unnecessary suffering the current approach to domestic abuse can have on everyone involved - including the children. If I hadn't recorded our abuser, they would have the kids now, bringing them up to be the next abusers or victims, and I would have been dead - as planned."

We join this story as Victim and Abuser happily get together, and follow the increasingly disturbing events that lead to the day Abuser tried to psycho glass Victim in the shower then vanish the children. That was the day of Abuser's second arrest and removal from the family home – never to legally return. But even court orders and further arrests didn't stop their campaign of hatred and hell. To this day, they still gaslight Victim for it all and claim to have been set up, something you can judge for yourself.

Abuse is not a gendered crime it is abuse, pure and simple. Male and female perpetrators behave far more similarly than you might think. In every case, it is about control over another – even if that means weaponising the children and murder by 'accident' or suicide. Think you know about real domestic abuse? Think again.

If you are a victim or survivor, regardless of gender, you have our empathy and support. People are dying and children are growing to become abusers or victims themselves. We all need to be heard louder, to break the cycle.

At the end of this book, there are three extra chapters:

Chapter A talks about **Johnny Depp**.

Chapter B gives an overview of **John's story**.

Chapter C looks at the **Duluth model**.

Moving, thought provoking, infuriating and upsetting, the victim's journey becomes one we share. One to help us better understand the hidden hell victims of abuse find themselves in, behind closed doors.

Contents

Chapter 1

How the Abuse Started

"I had been lied to"

14 years before escape

Victim says:

"If your partner has a personality disorder, can you ever really know them? Twenty years ago, when I first met Abuser, I thought the outbursts against their music partner were just them being artistically passionate. How naïve I was.

It was 1999 and I was living in Poland, teaching English and about to start making low-budget, feature-length films. Met as a friend of a friend, Abuser was lovely at first. We became friends, then best friends, talking about shared experiences of loss of a loved one. The partner I went to Poland for had walked out believing the lie of a friend, Abuser's had moved to Australia and we trauma bonded over this. I fell deeply in love and Abuser said they loved me too, though now I wonder if they ever really did."

After two years as best friends, Abuser moved into Victim's rented flat and things quickly began to change.

"I returned from finishing my summer job, teaching English in England, to find a red letter from the telephone company, threatening to cut us off for non-payment. The amount wasn't huge but I wanted to know why Abuser hadn't paid or at least told me it needed paying so I could. They told me, adamantly and straight to my face, that it was a mistake and they had paid it."

A common trait with narcissists is their ability to lie very, very well. So well they can even begin to believe their own lies - for these lies portray them as good, with everyone else as wrong.

"I loved Abuser and believed them. They stayed at home while I went to the telephone company to sort out the company's mistake, only it wasn't their mistake. Truly believing Abuser, I was as adamant to them as Abuser had been to me, repeating it had been paid, no matter what their computer said. I was adamant until they pulled out the paper-based logs of all payments for our flat and proved there was no such payment. Shocked, I apologised, paid the bill and went home with the cold realisation I had been lied

to."

To an outsider, it can seem senseless for people to stay with liars or abusers. A common trait victims have is a tolerant, forgiving nature – as well as the desire, even the need, to remain in the relationship, for what ever reason. Those suffering a psychological trait known as co-dependency, where they focus more on the welfare of others than themselves, are particularly at risk.

"When I got home, I could see on their face they knew I had found out. *'Why lie? Why didn't you just tell me?'* I asked. They said they didn't have the money to pay and had been too embarrassed to say. As angry and disappointed as I was, I understood how it felt to be broke. We hugged and the moment passed. We stayed together."

The standard pattern with abusers is to start out lovely and hook the victim with good experiences. Once hooked, step by step, the abuse begins. In Abuser's case, Victim tolerating and forgiving the lie, assured them they were both wanted and able to get away with bad behaviour. In many cases, when abusers add a 'pull them back', an 'excuse'; like words of love or a tears to invoke sympathy or pity. Crocodile tears remain a narcissistic abuser's favourite, regardless of gender.

"I had often seen Abuser shouting at their music partner but they had never shouted at me before. I don't remember the first time it happened but it was within months of us living together. What I remember very specifically was their being upset while they shouted. Their raging, red face streaked with tears. Rather than being focused on outrage at being yelled at, I felt sorry for them."

Victim has demonstrated co-dependency. Feeling the need to help Abuser at the expense of their own well being.

Once an abuser has tested the water and got away with it, the behaviour becomes the relationship's norm. Once normalised, the abuses become stronger and expand to take on other forms. Physical, psychological, coercion and outright threats, even against family and friends. All the while there will be the accompanying sympathy hold; in Abuser's case, their tear-streaked face as they blame Victim for making them feel so upset that they 'had' to shout and treat them that way.

"I knew Abuser was now dependent on me for accommodation so didn't feel able to just kick them out. Yet that winter, after the first ever six-hour argument of my life – I say argument, I mean waves of ranting – I wanted them gone. Even when I just tried to get away and go to sleep, they followed - throwing glass bottles at

my head as I lay there. It's the closest I've ever come to killing someone. I wanted them gone. If I could have thought of a way of disposing of the body, I possibly would have. That is how bad it was."

And still Victim let them stay. Logically this makes no sense but many such victims do – often for reasons they don't understand themselves – saying things like:

"Because I still loved them and at other times it was great, especially in public. Everyone thought we were the perfect couple and to others, at least when I was present, they spoke very highly of me, which felt good."

One of the things I read in Victim here are the insecurities. The lack of self-worth and not believing they deserved anything better. From Abuser's point of view, seeing how much they appreciates kind words, Victim has further identified themselves as someone who will tolerate bad behaviour. Victim is co-dependent on Abuser – through and through.

Chapter 2

Let's Finish

"Sex was one of the best things between us."

10 years before escape

By 2003, with the arguments almost daily and rages now involving smashing household objects, including a window when a thrown mug narrowly missed Victim's head, they decided to end it.

"Abuser's rages had been getting to me so much I smashed my phone in caged-animal frustration. Then I just woke up one sunny spring morning, sat on the edge of the bed and told Abuser, almost laughing at the obviousness of my realisation: *'This isn't working. Let's finish and just be friends'*. Abuser wasn't happy with that. They said: *'If we finish now it will mean we spent 18-months together for nothing. Let's try a bit longer.'*"

Once a narcissist has found a victim tolerant enough to stand their rages, they don't want to lose them, especially if the victim is seen as someone with potential for the riches and status they crave. In fact, as Victim would discover from a diary entry after their divorce, Abuser's motive for staying was not love but to go to England to make £50,000. With narcissists it is always about what you can do for them, voluntarily or otherwise.

"I could see they needed more time so said OK, thinking we would stay together for another month or two and then part as friends, having really tried our best."

Victim was blind to Abuser's true motives. What happened next? Did they then separate?

"Two months later, there was pregnancy."

Despite all the conflict, they had been having sex three times a day from the beginning, without protection as they both felt old enough to have a child. No pregnancy had happened for almost two years so they thought they couldn't have children. It turned out they could – apparently thanks to a further experiment in sexual positions, involving a chair.

"Sex was one of the best things between us. On this front we were very compatible and would fuck like rabbits. When learnt of the pregnancy parental instincts kicked. Actually glad to discover could have a child. They were Catholic and I wanted our child to have a British passport so marriage and a return to England was

the automatic next step."

There is no greater biological hook between a couple than a child. A narcissist, male or female, will be pleased to gain a hook as strong as this. It doesn't mean they will change their ways or do anything not focused on themselves, it just gives them more security and leverage to stop their chosen victim from escaping. Given this, you may think Abuser deliberately wanted to trap Victim but their diary revealed they didn't.

"Three days before our wedding, in my home town of Canterbury after another tear-streaked rant, I remember going for a walk by myself, thinking of calling the whole thing off. But Abuser was from Latvia and this was 2003, before Eastern Europeans had automatic right to reside in the UK. If we didn't get married Abuser would go back to Latvia, to a location I didn't know. I would never be the hands-on dad I had always planned to be, to make up for the lack of contact with my own father. There was no option but to go through with it."

Yes, Abuser is female. For Victim, the pregnancy became the unavoidable event. The marriage went ahead and they began a new life in England, initially staying with Victim's mother and stepfather. Victim taught English in Canterbury but, as his summer placement finished, tensions in the house rose then exploded - with stepdad throwing a suitcase thrown on their bed giving two weeks-notice to find somewhere else. Victim was offered permanent teaching work, to start after Christmas, yet this was too late to save their situation. Victim had a friend in Coventry so this is where they went to make their new life.

After a few weeks in Coventry, Victim got a job in a call-centre and got them a house. Sadly, Abuser's rages continued, even after the birth, and now they had two to abuse, with the infant hook to keep Victim there – chasing them around the house, shouting at the top of their voice, as Victim carried infant Paul, trying to save them both from the rages.

For an abuser, the location of the house was a God-send. On one side a mostly empty residence and on the other a mostly empty live music room of an Irish pub. Abuser could rant to their heart's content and, by all accounts, they did.

"Thinking breast feeding would stop another pregnancy and with sex the one thing Abuser never argued about, a second child was conceived – Alan was born just over a year after Paul. The first Father's Day present was a positive pregnancy test."

Now with two children between them, Abuser had an even deeper hook into Victim, which they took full advantage of. In 2005, when Victim had

9

moved on to well-paid TV work, Abuser was mostly happy. They could finally live like the royalty they believed they were. When this freelance work wasn't available, for that was the nature of the work, Victim was considered, as Abuser would put it: *"You're like a piece of shit under my shoe."*

Chapter 3

Their Parents

"Two years after marrying, I met their parents for the first time.

8 years before escape

"Like many people, I always thought I had a good childhood. Although after two years of therapy I more fully understood myself more and the influences of early childhood on my adult life. My very earliest memory is being breast fed – more exactly my deciding to stop suckling one day as stopped liking the taste. Mum told me I was six months old then. I also have a memory of playing alone in the back garden of our house, when I was two. Don't remember what my elder sister was doing but I was by myself. Had no connection with my dad, who didn't know how to play with children after a harsh childhood with his dad. Mum would have been busy looking after our sickly younger sister - who I thought was going to die."

This alone time was the beginning of Victim's feelings of abandonment and not belonging - which became their lifescript. It was also the beginning of their co-dependency, focused on loving and helping others as a way of feeling belonging.

"Growing up, this younger sister developed some real anger issues - perhaps because of what she suffered in infancy. She would start an attack against me but, if I then retaliated, it was always me who got told off. Nobody cared she had started it and this became another 'truth' in my life - that I couldn't get justice. My reaction was to withdraw and defended myself with distance – focusing instead on one or two close friends, with a romantic notion of having a partner to share things with. My first 'serious' partner was Samantha, when I was five. As infants, we used to walk to Beauherne school by ourselves and I would meet Samantha on the way. We became very close, never argued - just enjoyed our time together; until one day, out of the blue, Samantha arrived at our meeting point later than usual. Arrived in a red, four-door Ford Cortina saloon - I'll never forget that view. They got out and ran over to me but not to walk to school. *"We're moving away. I came to say goodbye."* I was so upset and shocked I don't remember even saying a word in reply and didn't return their wave as they got back in the car and was driven away.

I just watched as my best friend left, feeling sad and alone again. Still brings a tear to my eye writing this, almost 50 years later."

Abandonment again. A reinforcing of Victim's feelings of 'not belonging'. In adult life, still with this as a subconscious core belief, was why Victim still strove to make things work with Abuser. Feeling sorry for their tear-streaked face, even when they were attacking. Totally ignoring what they were suffering for, as life had taught, they didn't deserve anything better. And that is how the narcissist was able to take advantage - mistaking kindness for weakness.

"Not long after Samantha left, possibly inspired by watching International Rescue in Thunderbirds, I decided on my life's aim: to have a positive impact on the world. Part of that included always showing a smile to those around me – to help others feel happier, which made me feel happier too."

Psychologically, this smile is called a mask. It isn't a reflection of how Victim is really feeling but of what they want to 'wear' on their face. It also indicates a subconscious detachment and denial of the deeper, painful feelings. The co-dependency now strongly in evidence - giving a smile to make others smile, regardless of how lost or abandoned they felt inside.

"Dad died when I was 17. He'd been diagnosed with lung cancer 13-months earlier. It was ironic because until I was about 15 we hadn't really known him. He was always too busy with work or away in the pub in the evenings. Talking to my mum in 2019, I learnt he had tried playing with us when we were kids but, when I was just two years old, apparently I punched him in the face – possibly because he was being too rough. He punched me in the face back and that was the last time I wanted to play with him. Maybe that is why I grew up feeling he was angry with having kids, at least until I was 15. Then he got a new job and the family house he and mum had been building was completed and everything became happy. We started spending time together – until I came home from the cinema to have my happy world broken again. He'd fallen off a ladder and was in hospital. I had been talking with him about the film, First Blood, before I left and now he was in Maidstone hospital. Not long after, the X-rays revealed he had lung cancer. After 13-months of us all actively not talking about it, we lost him. Now I'm tearful again."

The lack of communication and closeness in the family unit while growing up, had only increased Victim's sense of needing to belong. Building not just an ever stronger co-dependency but also a need to build thier own family. To have their own kids and be close to them, in the way their parents didn't know how to be.

"About a year after dad died, trying to find closeness with a friend, I asked them out. They turned me down. So sad, I went to a pub, got hammered on vodka and literally ran home, intent on killing myself with dad's WWII bayonet. The only thing that stopped me, as I sat holding it in my room crying, was the upset I knew it would have given mum, so soon after losing dad."

This was a positive impact of co-dependency. Putting their mother's feelings above their own saved their life.

"In 2005, two years after marrying Abuser and now with two infant boys, I met their parents for the very first time. I had been doing investigative work for TV so financially we were very OK. While this removed Abuser's ability to nag about money, it didn't stop them nagging about other things.

It was a 2,000 mile drive to south-eastern Latvia, near the border with the Russian Federation. In Germany, we had been going quickly, comfortably cruising at over 110mph in the fastest car I'd ever owned. At 5am I pulled over for a catnap, only to find Abuser nagging me, saying: 'You need to sleep in a hotel'. Knowing myself, having driven solo across the continent several times before, I knew they were wrong but they just wouldn't give up or shut up. In the end I abandoned the nap idea and drove on, now over-tired but fully awake with anger. An hour later we were doing 145mph near Berlin, kids sleeping in the back. Just 12 hours after leaving Coventry in England, we hit the Polish border near Wrocław and the effect of new EU funding: masses of roadworks – sometimes even missing roads. We stayed in a Polish hotel before continuing. What should have taken another day took over two."

As Abuser had totally refused to listen to what Victim wanted to do sleep wise, we can see it was not their concern for them to sleep in a hotel but a projection - they wanted the comfort of a hotel. If it had been a genuine concern for Victim would they not have at least stopped nagging so Victim could take a nap? The fact they didn't simply confirms it was about their wants, not Victim's.

"Three days after leaving home in England, after some of the worst roads I'd ever seen, we arrived in Latvia's second city, Daugavpils; in one of the poorest parts of Europe. Daugavpils presented itself as the ex-Soviet city it was, a few grandiose

buildings yet mostly grey apartment blocks and rundown, partially collapsed houses, trams and pot-hole road-system mayhem. I met their parents for the first time, which was pleasant and welcoming and then, literally within an hour of arriving, Abuser was already volunteering me to drive to other relatives. They didn't, for one second, consider that I could be tired. Not one. What was more important was wasting not time to show off we had a nice car and two lovely boys. Compared to everyone else, they felt like royalty from England and wanted to revel in it."

And there we have the full answer, regarding empathy and concern. If Abuser had any for Victim's welfare they would have let them take a break from driving. Instead, they valued the materialism and higher-status ego boost, focusing on these needs not Victim's. Standard, narcissist behaviour.

"Staying with Abuser's parents, even on that first day I noticed their mother was verbally aggressive towards their father. Although in Latvia, as they were of Polish decent, their main language was Polish, followed by Russian. I spoke some Polish as that was where I lived with Abuser before the pregnancy. Within days I heard Abuser's mother shouting at thir dad, word for word, what Abuser shouted at me in England: *'Jesteś pjani yak swińka!'* (you are drunk like a pig), even though he wasn't. Unlike me, their father was only too ready to automatically shout back.

For me it was a lightbulb moment, suddenly explaining where Abuser had learnt it was 'normal' to shout at a spouse and for the spouse to shout back. I hadn't grown up like that and refused to behave that way - when Abuser shouted at me I refused to shout back. Their response? Not happiness at the calm but to call me heartless, like a stone and uncaring. How ridiculous is that? Especially as Abuser had told me how, as a child, they used to lock themselves in the bathroom and run the shower to block out the noise of their parent's shouting because they hated it so much. Rather than save our children from such a fate, they seemed determined to repeat it."

Domestic violence has a devastating impact on children and young people that can last into adulthood.

Women's Aid website, 2019.

I find it amazing that Women's Aid, while stating they recognise the devastating impact of domestic abuse on the children, seem more than happy to actively work against male victims and, as a direct consequence, further the abuse the children by keeping them with an abusive mother.

14

Why keep children prisoners in homes of abuse, making them grow up psychologically damaged and likely to repeat the cycle by becoming co-dependent victims or narcissistic abusers themselves, as did Abuser?

"From time to time, Abuser got a cold-sore on their lip. What I never understood and still don't to this day is that they chose to kiss baby Alan while the virus was active. I watched stunned as they gave him a quick kiss on the lips but physically stopped them as they went to kiss his eyes. I couldn't believe it. Did they want to make him blind? While glad I stopped them from kissing his eye, they still passed on the virus to his lips – something he and my conscience will have to live with for the rest of our lives."

> **Domestic violence is a gendered crime...**
> **Women's Aid** website, 2019

To me this is another Women's Aid myth, in keeping with the Duluth model and a key mantra they use to increase their funding. In factual reality, abuse is only a gendered crime in the sense that, all too often, female abusers are not just permitted but even helped to get away with it - at the expense of everyone around them, children included. Male refuges, where are they? Male victim support? It's struggling to exist, even in 2025.

Abuse is a crime, pure and simple, regardless of gender. I challenge anyone, female-centric NGOs and government bodies included, to deny it should be treated as such.

Chapter 4

Abuser's Detective, Part 1

"Abuser was always jealous I'd had more partners"

7 years before escape

"Abuser and I went to a sex-focused club called Scarlet's, as a treat for their 30th birthday. As a couple we were very open about sex – the best connection in our relationship and not shy about it either. We both dressed up as nurses and, as underwear-free Abuser was bending over a 'chair' some stranger knelt down had started licking their crotch. I wasn't jealous. Such possibilities had been agreed and it was that kind of event – just went to their face and asked if they were OK about it. They were surprised: "I thought it was you", and wanted it stopped so I told the person time out. They did stop but it didn't stop Abuser taking their number and spending the next few months complaining to them about me when they were angry, which was often. They also learnt this person had been falsely accused of rape, by a vindictive ex - which had made their life hell for three days, with no action taken against the ex for the lie. Abuser never forgot that, as I would find out in the year of escape.

One summer evening, Abuser vanished. I didn't know where they had gone, beyond saying they would travel to nearby Leamington Spa where their nephew lived. When they got back, annoyed and disappointed four hours later, they told me they had gone to various pubs, looking for someone I'll abbreviate to 'W', from their previous job in Banbury. We had been together for six years by then and, due to their aggressions, if they had told me they were leaving for someone else, I would have helped them pack and given my blessing.

As far as I knew that was that, but eight years later, while sorting through Abuser's abandoned possessions, I found some notebooks, diaries and a couple of emails they had printed off at the time."

From Abuser's 2007 notebook, repeated on several pages across it:

'Radość życia, gdzie ty?'

"It translates to: 'Happy life, where are you?'"

Hi, it was good talking to you on Friday. As promised here are the details of the person I am looking for:

'W' XXXX,

Was born in 1983 or 1984 (probably July) and I don't know where but is a holder of a British passport.

During the last year they lived in Banbury (Oxfordshire), I think with their sister or some relative. From September 2006 until May 2007 they worked at XXXX near Banbury. Their previous work is: XXXX

Their old personal number is 0790 XXXX....

I have no idea what else is needed in order to find them, so please let me know if this information is enough to track someone down...

I also rely a lot on your confidentiality and please tell me when and how I should pay you for the service I look forward to hearing from you. Thanks a lot.

Abuser

"Confidential? Confidentiality of what? Their firm intention to be unfaithful to me?"

Email Abuser printed, of 4ᵗʰ November 2007, from the detective agency:

Dear Abuser,

I have received this email from you and can start work to find 'W' XXXX if you require. Usually we find most people within 7-28 days. There seems sufficient information in order to locate them. To proceed we require a deposit of £117.50 (including VAT) and balance is payable only when we complete the job. The total amount would be in the region of £250 plus VAT.

Regards,

Peter.

...papers regarding Las Vegas and 'W'.

...I wish you were still in Banbury – it's the closest to the place I got stuck in my life.... you might be Cancer (star sign), love to sixty-nine position, Happy Birthday!, if I am right and... I am missing you...I still dare to want you....I would not mind celebrating the forth coming National Orgasm Day with you, the closest to French, black and shaven thing I can send you without risking my job...

Group sex, ejaculation on face or body is called Bukkake....

'W'... I love them.

Since I've missed both kissing and Nationals Days to use as excuses for getting in touch with you...

Victim is this kind of person with whom I will never be able to buy a house or make some kind of move. They are obsessed with their film stuff.

"Abuser was always jealous I'd had more partners before we got together and, going by this, it is clear they were intending to up their count, maybe had already been been upping it."

Chapter 5

First Police

"Abuser remained furious for being arrested"

6 years before escape

25th November 2007.

"To say life with Abuser was challenging is quite an understatement. Once back in England, married with two young children, their rants and rages had been getting progressively worse. One of my escapes was to try and drink myself to happiness, in my office corner upstairs. On this occasion, and I can admit it makes me partly to blame, it was the night before our kids were due to go to a birthday party. Desperate for a psychological escape from Abuser's rants though, I felt the need to get drunk. To compromise, trying to still be a responsible parent, I first sat down with Abuser and went through the directions for them to drive them there, in the car I had bought and collected for them, with a loan from my mother. They saw the party location on the map, said they understood where it was and how to get there. Feeling I had done my duty, I went to work on my computer and got drunk. The next morning, it all kicked off."

There is a common behaviour in victims of domestic violence, the numbing or avoiding of the pain, as they feel unable to change the cause of the pain: the behaviour of their abuser and their response to it. This is a coping mechanism and the numbing can involve drugs, alcohol and other forms of self-harm. Actual avoiding is another coping mechanism, which can range from simply leaving the home for a while to leaving overnight or working away; basically being anywhere but in the home with the abuser.

"I got woken by Abuser raging about running late for the party and not knowing where to go and that I should drive them there. I wasn't in a fit state to drive anywhere and reminded Abuser I had explained where to go the night before. That wasn't what they wanted to hear. Their rage got worse and they lashed out, throwing shoes at my face."

Narcissistic rage is rarely red-mist, mindless lashing out. It is a cold, focused outburst of anger to put the other down - where the only limits on how far they will go are how much they think they can get away with. Such narcissistic rages can become so destructive they become a personality disorder, so called because they disorder the person's life. Throwing shoes at Victim's face, if not a definitive sign of a disorder is certainly a sign of rage.

"Being hit in the face by shoes, for no good reason, hurt and really annoyed me. As I leapt up, Abuser ran downstairs saying they were going to call the police, which was ridiculous. I ran after them and grappled for the phone now in their hand. I knew how well they lied and the last thing I wanted was having to spend hours disputing things with the police."

This is the behavioural trait amongst abusers mentioned before, called DARVO (Deny Attack and Reverse Victim and Offender), where the abuser manipulates the account of events to make them appear the victim. It seems Victim is aware they are likely to do something like this.

"As we grappled, Abuser lashed out – hitting me in the face again, this time with the receiver. That really hurt. I left the struggle and went back upstairs, no longer caring if they called the police or not."

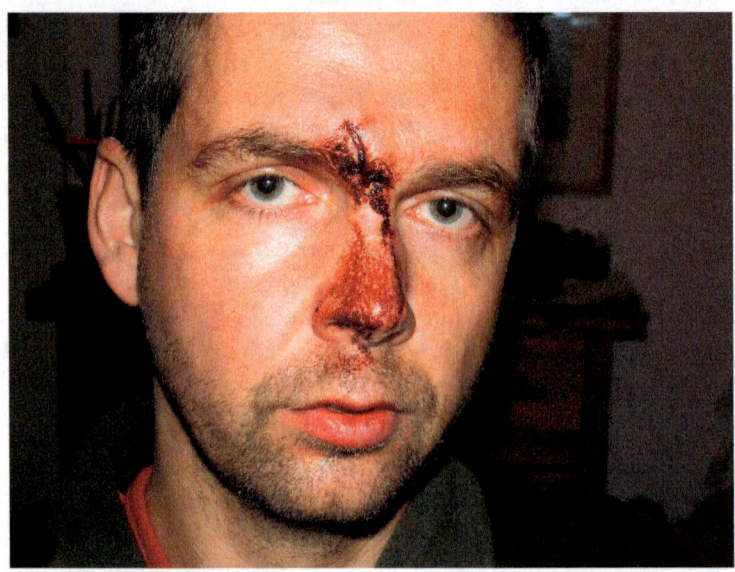

After domestic abuse that day

If Abuser had really feared for their safety, now alone they had the perfect opportunity to call the police. They didn't. What does that say? To me is says it was simply a threat, as part of coercive control.

"When I got up again, an hour later, Abuser had gone to the party with the kids. It was then that I caught sight of the cut and dried blood on my face. A cut and bloodied face? This really

annoyed me. I had put up with so much abuse but drew the line at being bloodied. Wanting it officially logged, now I was the one phoning the police, then got dressed and walked to the central police station to give a statement."

Police control centre log, 25/11/2007, 13:24

Incident detail: CALLER HAS BEEN ATTACKED BY SPOUSE – THEY HAS NOW LEFT THE H/A... CHILDREN PRESENT DURING THE ATTACK AND THEY HAVE NOW LEFT... CHILDREN ARE 3YRS AND 4YRS... CALLER HAS FACIAL INJURIES NO AMBO REQUIRED

Incident Result: REPORT - CRIME

One of the things misunderstood, about domestic violence victims left too long in harm's way, is how the psychological pain and harm can build to breaking point. An attack can make victims suddenly explode, in a burst of pent up anger that can ultimately lead to murder.

Only since 2015 has UK law recognised the offence of coercive and controlling behaviour as a crime. Though it is very rarely acted upon, for how to prove it? Even if a victim makes a complaint, unless there is a pile of evidence to support it, the abuser can simply lie their way out, especially if supported by the myth that only males abuse.

At best it ends in a draw, with no action being taken either way – in other cases, if the abuser is a sobbing female adamant they are the victim, action will almost certainly be taken against their male victim; further abusing the real victim and further empowering the abuser.

"With blood on my face, the police actually took my report seriously. I didn't want to press charges, I just wanted something on the system to log their abusive ways. To my surprise, the police took me home so I could look after the kids while they arrested Abuser, recently returned from the party. *'How could you?'***, Abuser glared as they led them away. I had never intended to get them arrested - it was something else I didn't want that was unable to control. Could only watch as they were taken away and then go to look after the kids, wondering how terrible they would be when they got back."**

This is real issue with domestic violence victims where, even if they dare go to the police for help, they are then faced with their abuser returning home, with all the fury they will have for being arrested. For this reason, in 2014 the UK government introduced DVPOs (domestic violence protection orders) and DVPNs (domestic violence protection notices), designed to prevent abusers returning to the family home if needs be. DVPNs can be applied by the police

21

with immediate effect, if deemed it necessary - even if there is no evidence against the accused. In theory, these are a really good idea. In practice, with abuser abilities to DARVO the situations, in many police forces 100% of these orders are applied against males. Rather than protecting victims, these orders can all to often end up further empowering abusers, for now their victims can be losing their home, with children left with the real abuser. Very often, the only way back is to kowtow to the abuser's increased demands - needing their 'kindness' to be allowed back.

Police log, 25/11/2007, 16.55

On Sunday 25th November 2007, I attended North Road to speak with a female I now know as Abuser FORD.

Abuser FORD was named as being responsible for a domestic assault in which Victim FORD had reported on the same day Abuser had assaulted them by throwing a child's shoe directly at their face causing an approx 1" cut to their face.

At 16.55hrs on this day I said to Abuser FORD, "I AM ARRESTING YOU ON SUSPICION OF ASSAULT, CAUTION, IT IS NECESSARY TO ARREST YOU TO ALLOW A FULL AND PROMPT INVESTIGATION OF THE OFFENCE"

FORD made no reply and was conveyed to Central Police Station where their detention was authorised.

"Abuser returned home several hours later, surprisingly subdued. Rather than ranting there was a mixture of quiet fury and upset. Angry I had dared to do it to them and feeling very sorry for themself, though not at all sorry for the inch-long cut on my head or their aggressions that had triggered their arrest in the first place. They kept asking how I was able to call the police - seeming to forget they had been the one who had first tried getting the police involved. Apparently the police had tried to get them to accept a Caution but they had refused, no doubt adamant they not at fault for anything – with me not pressing charges the whole matter was dropped. By the next day, subdued Abuser had gone and abusive Abuser was back."

Hitler was once asked how he got people to follow his thinking. He replied: *'People will believe anything you say, if you say it forcefully enough.'* From what I have seen, narcissistic abusers use a similar technique – partly because they actually start to believe the lies they repeatedly tell.

"Days later, Abuser got a letter from the police, reminding them of they arrest and their need to behave. That made them furious.

They tore it up and had another rant at me. Who ever decided such things are a good idea has never lived with domestic abuse. Days after that, there came a knock at the door. Two police officers, come to make sure everything was OK - good intentions but when you live with an abuser, all things like this do are antagonise and infuriate them. The very nature of domestic abuse is that it is in your home, 24/7. There is no escape. There are no witnesses - no safeguards. You are privately caged with the animal so how is antagonising it then waltzing away and leaving you to deal with the consequences supposed to help? If they had fear of the law or even regard for it, they wouldn't be abusive in the first place."

One of the mistakes the authorities seem to make regarding domestic violence is thinking they are dealing with people who can be reasoned with. Abusers, by their very nature, are not reasonable people.

"Abuser remained furious for being arrested and repeatedly threatened revenge. Four months later they got it, though probably not quite as expected."

Chapter 6

Abuser's Detective, Part 2

"Logging in, I changed their height to 5'0" and weight to 170lb"

5 years before escape

"Along with the other emails Abuser had printed, I also discovered these in 2015."

Email, printed 23rd January 2008, to the detective agency:

Dear Peter,

Hope you had a good Christmas. Is there any news regarding 'W'?

Please let me know if there is any problem to find him. Thanks.

Abuser.

Email, printed 23rd January 2008, from the detective agency:

Dear Abuser,

I have tried to call you several times in order to discuss this case with you and confirm some details. The information I have come up with so far is:

'W' XXXX

XXXX Banbury, Oxfordshire, OX16 XXX

Living with XXX, Derek (same surname) and two women with the surname Simms – XXXX and XXXX. Do you think this is the right one? Do you know their sister's name at all?

Regards,

Peter.

"I didn't find any more such emails printed off but did find a street map of Banbury, with the address given by Peter circled. Our relationship was not good and I knew in the summer of 2007 that Abuser was interested in someone at work. They told me they had been turned down because they were married, which made them more angry with me as I was now blamed me 'W' turning them down. Everything always my fault, even the failure of their attempts at infidelity.

Finding these emails illustrated just how two-faced Abuser was when falsely accusing me of an affair in 2012. They also verified their determination to have affairs, in this case paying over £250 to a private detective to find 'W'. In 2013, after their arrest and removal from our house, I discovered they had joined the Ashley Maddison dating agency, with the user name: Bored with my Spouse. At the time I had access to their account as we had installed a keylogger on their laptop to monitor our kids – which they had forgotten about. Their typing, including password, had been emailed to me in the automatic reports. Seeing what was going on, I logged in and changed their height to 5'0" (150cm) and their weight to 170lb (77kg), nothing else - doing this actually made me smile. By now I really didn't care who they slept with."

This is especially important for what will happen in 2012, after Victim secretly visits a friend in Kraków.

Chapter 7

Victim's Arrest

"Abuser saw the look on my face and knew they had gone too far"

19th March 2008.

"We didn't live in the best part of Coventry and some vandals had damaged a few cars, including smashing a window on mine, so I had put up CCTV. It was this CCTV that captured some of what was to happen this evening."

With the ability to lie so passionately, very often the only way to really prove what happens during a domestic dispute is recorded evidence – though doing so can create risks in itself.

"Abuser had been shouting at me in the car with the kids even before we got home. I just wanted an escape, went upstairs to my computer corner, turned it on and started drinking. Abuser followed, not wanting to lose their verbal punchbag."

Psychologically, narcissistic abusers are very unhappy inside. Rather than admit and deal with their inner demons, often from early infancy, they project their anger and failings on others, to try and make themselves feel better - but it can never fix their inner pain for they are refusing to even acknowledge it. Take their victim, their external anger focus, away and they are left floundering. To avoid this loss of rage outlet, if the victim runs away, they go after them.

"Every time Abuser returned to launch another furious rant, I would do my best to ignore it and focus on what I was doing to reduce the psychological impact. I knew they wanted a shouting match, in the footsteps of their parents, and that it would resolve nothing for they didn't want a solution, just war against me. Shouting was not my way or the way I wanted our kids to see us, so I refused to engage until they talked reasonably. The recording shows they did for a while then, when not getting the answers they wanted, went back to raging. As Abuser came to the doorway, ranting behind me and getting themselves more and more wound up, I drank harder, to numb the pain."

Although we can see Victim's drinking alcohol is not going to resolved anything, is there anything they could have done that would? Along with physical avoidance the drinking is a coping mechanism for the pain.

"Abuser had been shouting at me, off and on, for over three hours and had still failed to get me to shout back, even after throwing a clock at my head – which missed by a whisker and bounced off the wall in front of my face. I still have this clock.

The next thing I knew they were pouring a large tin of white emulsion over me, my computer, my cameras, my entire work area. Telling me it was my fault for not doing what they wanted. I couldn't believe it, dropping to my hands and knees to try and rescue my equipment. To rescue my upset, I opened a bottle of home-made wine, a present from another parent. Which I admit was not the best thing to do."

The partially rescued home office after Abuser's paint attack

It is a standard abuser trait, to attack the victim then blame them for it, with zero empathy or remorse for any pain caused. Perhaps Abuser was even finding pleasure in it.

"As I was on my hands and knees, working to rescue my digital cameras and computer equipment now drowning in paint, Abuser came back, stood in the doorway and announced: *'If you don't do what I say now, I'll do something worse'*. Worse? I snapped. I couldn't take worse. I got to my feet and I went for them."

With very few exceptions, situations like this can result in the victim going overboard and even being imprisoned for it, with all the cruelty and abuse that brought it on going unrecognised.

"Abuser saw the look on my face and knew they had gone too far - they ran across the landing to our bedroom and I went after them – knowing I was going to hit them. Near the top of the stairs between the rooms was Alan, our youngest son then aged three. Afraid he might panic and fall down the stairs with what I was going to do, I picked him up and held him in one hand as I went to Abuser and, for the first time in my life, punched such a person in the face. What surprised me most was not so much how soft their face felt against my fist but how much I wanted to do it. Now I was the one shouting: *FUCK OFF! LEAVE ME ALONE! DON'T YOU EVER TOUCH MY STUFF AGAIN!'* I don't remember ever being so angry with anyone before. Outburst over and point made, I put down our crying son and returned to my paint-drowning things. Abuser, without another word to me, went downstairs and called the police.

I feel no guilt for hitting Abuser but terrible guilt for the horror Alan must have felt while I was doing it – even though he says has no memory of it now. As for Abuser, I felt angry they had pushed me to that point. Took years of therapy to get over that feeling.

When Abuser told me they had called the police, I just sighed and waited for their arrival. Predicting unfair treatment, I tried to activate a tiny voice recorder, though was too drunk to get it to work. When I saw the police cars arrive, blue lights flashing, I opened the door to the two female officers knocking on it, probably looking like some drunk decorator as I was covered in white paint. One went further inside and appeared shortly after with Abuser, blood on their lip. I was arrested and marched outside, in handcuffs, hands behind my back. Outside the officer pushed me against our garden wall, and put her arm across my throat. If there hadn't been so many other officers watching, she would probably have done something more. Instead she then stuffed me in the back of her squad car, saying: *'You like hitting them, do you'*, and, out of sight of any others, reached behind my back to give the handcuffs a painful twist. Exactly the kind of behaviour I had been wanting to record and felt annoyed that I wasn't. At least the CCTV watching my car recorded her arm across my throat."

Police log, 19th March 2008, by arresting officer

Abuser was crying and I could see that their lower lip on their mouth was split and was bleeding.

I said "What has happened?"

Abuser has replied "Victim has kicked me in the mouth".

I have then said "How many times."

Abuser has replied "They kicked me once right in the mouth"

I have then gone into the front room and said to Victim FORD "You are under arrest on suspicion of assault (CAUTION) This arrest is necessary to allow the prompt and effective of this offence"

FORD has replied "You shouldn't be arresting me you should arrest my spouse. They have assaulted me - look at my face and all the cuts."

FORD has no visible cuts.

I have placed them in handcuffs to the rear for my own safety and PC XXXX, they have then been placed in a marked police vehicle and transported to Central Police Station.

During the booking in process FORD has been taken straight to a cell due to their behaviour.

I have had no further dealings with FORD

Quite what behaviour this officer is referring to is unclear. A later report states Victim punched not kicked Abuser. Victim's retaliatory assault on Abuser aside, which can be understood but never condoned, the CCTV evidence illustrates the only person with bad behaviour arrest wise was that officer herself.

CCTV footage from the front of their house, 19th March 2008

21.49.41, a squad car stops outside.

21.49.45, Victim can be heard saying: "They've arrived.", as two female officers get out.

21.50.07, officers heard knocking on the front door. Abuser doesn't open it, Victim does. Abuser can be heard talking to the three year old.

21.50.37, more squad cars arrive.

21.50.42, female officer heard calling "Hello. Police." up the stairs.

21.50.49, two male officers arrive at the open front door.

21.51.08, the two male officers leave the house.

21.51.32, a compliant Victim is led out of the house with hands cuffed behind their back by a female officer, who yanks them about and pins them against the garden wall with her forearm across their throat and aggressive body language towards them. Victim shows no sign of resistance, verbal or physical. The other female officer has gone to their squad car and not seen what is done behind her.

21.51.39, Victim is led towards the squad car and taken around the back of it to the left hand side where they are put inside.

21.51.02, with Victim now in the back of the car the two female officers exchange words outside it. The aggressive female officer then opens the right hand rear door and leans in close to Victim before getting in next to them, while the other returns to the house.

21.53,32, with Victim still alone in the back of the car with the aggressive officer, another squad car arrives and the other female officer leaves the house and gets into the drivers seat. There is some kind of an exchange between the officers and the aggressive one can be seen turning again towards Victim.

21.53.50, the three year old can be heard telling Abuser: "I'm waving to Victim." "Victim's going with the police.", is Abuser's nonplussed reply.

21.54.08, two squad cars and then two police vans, one transit sized, leave the scene.

Police log: Child Abuse and Domestic Violence Incident, reported 19 MAR 2018 21:48

Brief resume: Log 2XXXX & WcXXXX: FOLLOWING A VERBAL ARGUMENT AND WHILST DRUNK VICTIM HAS ASSAULTED THEIR SPOUSE BY PUNCHING TO THE FACE. IP WAS FRIGHTENED WHEN THEY SAW THAT THEY WERE BLEEDING. OFFENDER ARRESTED.

Repeat Victim: N *(No)*

Action No 1 Date 20-MAR-08

Notes: HIGH RISK. COPY FILE SENT TO HEALTH AND CAIU. INPUT FOR POLICE WATCH.

Action: NF *(No further action)*

DV Ltr Sent 28-MAR-08

Given the physicality of the incident it is entirely appropriate for such a log to be made. It is curious though, how Abuser is logged as only being frightened when saw the blood on their face, rather than of Victim themself.

Chapter 8

You Need Anger Management

"I know", Abuser

"I was really annoyed at what had happened. I had never punched a partner in my life, yet after 4 hours of verbal, psychological and then physical abuse, followed by a direct threat to do worse I had been abused to the point of explosion. All the police were looking at was the explosion. The self-appointed vigilante arresting officer had given some extra twists of the cuffs to inflict further pain on me – if she had the opportunity to do more have no doubt she would."

This is typical of abuse victims, pushed to the point of explosion, as Victim puts it, and lashing out to get their relentless attacker to finally back off. But the biggest evidence the police got presented with was sobbing Abuser with a physical injury so that was all they acted on. Of course, no-one can condone physical violence but just how much is any human being supposed to take, psychologically or physically, before they snap and explode? Without any such explosion when would Abuser have stopped? Would they have stopped? They weren't slowing down their attacks but escalating them. Without Victim's explosion would they have resorted to more assaults against them, possibly with a knife? If such abusers could listen to reason they wouldn't behave in such unreasonable ways in the first place. Ask yourself this, what would you do if someone had been shouting at you for four hours and then attacked you they way Abuser did?

Until 2015, there was no British law against psychological or coercive abuse. Unlike the case of Sally Challen, who murdered her abuser, Victim didn't try to kill Abuser. Victim retaliated, once, and then went back to trying to rescue their paint-soaked equipment. Absolutely none of this would have happened, not the attack against Abuser nor anything after, had it not been for their relentless aggression, rages, attacks and then threats of worse to come.

"In the morning, not trusting the system to be fair against victims, I got a solicitor and he advised me to go 'no comment', which I did. I felt stupid, as the officer performing the interview came across as a reasonable person, and I had to just sit there repeating: 'No comment.', even when asked: 'Do you intend to go no comment for everything?', I said 'No comment.' The only point I broke from this was when it came to my reason for staying with Abuser, our children. 'The children are fine.', said the officer,

'Thank you.', I replied, getting a frown from the solicitor. As when I went to the police about Abuser's assault months earlier, they weren't pressing charges against me either. Yet I was still kept in custody and put through the DNA swab and fingerprint routines of an arrestee."

In Victim's case, abusive Abuser didn't want to lose their verbal and psychological punchbag, knowing full well they were actually gentle and kind rather than violent in nature; that they had simply hammered them too far. Besides, Abuser finally had their revenge of getting Victim arrested too. Box ticked.

"After I had been dealt with for my actions, whilst still at the station, I put in a complaint against the arresting officer. She denied it and nothing came of it, apart from it being logged on her file should she do it again to someone else. If I had checked the CCTV footage earlier and seen the evidence it recorded, maybe something more would have happened. Either way, she is no longer a serving officer in that police unit. I have checked.

When I was released, I found Abuser sitting in the waiting area. They looked up at me as I was let out. They were calm and placid, with barely a mark on their lip. The only words I said to them were:

'You need anger management.'

They replied:

'I know.'

We left the police station together and tried to put it behind us."

Chapter 9

Laptop Launch

"I don't remember them ever saying thank you", Victim

<u>May 2008.</u>

"After Abuser's paint and clock throwing attacks in March, I had added an internal camera to the CCTV system, to record any further ones while at my computer. With Abuser refusing to get any anger management, things had got back to 'normal' pretty quickly and their temper outbursts remained. On this night, Abuser was sitting at their desk behind me, working on the laptop I had given them. I was working at my rebuilt office computer, can of cider nearby. I wasn't even tipsy yet Abuser still chose to wind themself up and kick off about things, including alcohol, which I always felt was unfair. If Abuser wanted a teetotaller, why did they choose someone who wasn't and then rage about it?"

Transcript, 21st May 2008, 1.19am, home office in front bedroom -

VICTIM	...that's your question, so why are you wearing white?
ABUSER	...your drinking just
VICTIM	Your excessive reaction
ABUSER	Come on. So let's...
	ABUSER SHOVES THEIR LAPTOP OFF THE DESK ONTO THE FLOOR, STANDS UP AND STRIDES OVER TO VICTIM
VICTIM	Abuser.
ABUSER	Yes. I don't have any reaction?
ABUSER	You're fucking closing this (computer) and talking to me.
VICTIM	I'm not going to agree with you. Koniec (The end).
ABUSER	You're fucking talking to me.
VICTIM	So I'm talking to you but I'm not agreeing with you.

"After Abuser calmed down, no doubt helped by knowing they were on camera, they went back to their desk and picked up their laptop. Then got angry again as it was broken – they had killed it."

Abuser demonstrates an almost total lack of control with their temper. I say almost because they demonstrate they can control it when they know their actions can be held to account, in this case via the internal CCTV camera now there to record further aggression.

"Luckily for Abuser, I was able to repair the laptop by putting in a new hard disk, operating system and software. Took several hours and cost me £100 for the disk yet I don't remember them ever saying thank you."

This is typical of Victim's co-dependency. Regardless of what is done against them, they still puts themself out for their Abuser. This is why such people are so popular with abusers and why abusers, for all the things they say and do against their victims, really don't want to lose them. Such tolerant, loving and self-sacrificing people are hard to find.

Abuser probably didn't say thank you because they blamed Victim for 'making' them angry in the first place.

Chapter 10

"You Fucking Ignored Me!"

'They're a bully', Abuser's best friend

"Summer 2008, Abuser's parents were having their Golden Wedding Anniversary and we drove the 2,000 miles to Latvia, at my expense. Abuser had a driving licence now but still wanted me to do all the driving again, which was fine but I did need to have good sleep before going - I didn't. Abuser wouldn't let me. Instead they demanded I help them with the preparations, right into the final hours before our night-time departure. I was under slept before we left and, despite the odd moments of sleep grabbed on the Channel crossing, in Germany it all caught up with me - to the point that I had to pull over every few hours to cat nap. Abuser found this frustrating and showed it. I found it annoying and predictable but if I was too tired to drive I was too tired to drive and would stop for a break. Thinking back on it, maybe this is what inspired Abuser to deny me sleep before the night driving jobs I had later.

We arrived in time for the wedding preparations and, despite the 2,000 miles I had just driven, Abuser again wasted no time volunteering me to taxi people around – while they enjoyed taking charge of the preparations.

Feeling ever more out of love with Abuser and totally fed up with being used and abused, I walked off - not knowing where I was going, literally. Probably embarrassed to have lost their spouse in front of so many relatives, Abuser sent their brother to come and find me. I got on really well with their family, even their shouting mother as they didn't shout at me. I was found, 'rescued' and driven back to the party, where people probably just thought I was glum from alcohol rather than my marriage and, when no-one else could hear, Abuser wasted no time scolding me for embarrassing them and telling me how glad I should be for them not telling their family I had 'hit' them in March. Lucky me...

With £22,000 borrowed from my mum and stepdad, we had bought a flat in the town and, a few days later, I went to stay there, buying enough alcohol on the way to sink an elephant – knowing no other way to numb the pain my life had become. Abuser's godmother, the only one I didn't really get on with for she felt compelled to believe every single thing Abuser said against me, including me being an alcoholic, took the opportunity to further that view and further pity Abuser for marrying me. I didn't care. I knew the truth of who I was, though also knew I was losing myself and my self-belief.

As much as your brain can logically remind you of being a good, talented, capable person – when your partner repeatedly calls you a talentless, worthless piece of shit that 'everyone' hates and 'nobody' likes or wants to work with – the negative seeps in. And, bit by bit, psychologically you lose yourself.

Back in England, in 2010, now in a bigger house in a better area for a 'new beginning' to our marriage, Abuser admitted they had some mental health issue and was thinking of getting some help. Just like their anger management, this didn't happen. A few weeks later, while I was with the children at the city's Memorial Park festival, Abuser left them with my mother and stormed home, bursting in the front door and up the stairs shouting: *'You Fucking Ignored Me!'* I didn't have a clue what they were on about – hadn't received any calls or texts from them. Believing I had been ignoring them, they grabbed my smartphone and threw it out the first floor window, where it smashed on the pavement outside. Used to such behaviour, my first reaction was to hurry outside and retrieve the pieces before they got walked on.

Abuser, getting even more furious as I was just being pragmatic about what they had done, stormed into my home office, now in a separate room and began trashing my things. I was determined to stop this and grabbed them. Against very, very determined resistance, I began physically pulling them out. In the struggle, they banged their head on the door frame. Realising they were hurt, I immediately stopped pulling, apologised and tried to help. Their response? *'If I have a brain problem now it's your fault'*. Everything was always my fault – regardless of anything they did against me.

Not long after this, struggling to cope with Abuser's behaviour, which our 'new-start house' had obviously failed to improve, I began confiding in their best friend and work colleague, Natasha - a Russian married to a British man with a young daughter. 'They're a bully.', concluded Natasha, in sympathy.

Chapter 11

Signs You're in an Abusive Relationship

"I had doubted justice for victims"

2 years before escape

"As clear as the answer would be to a fly on the wall, when you have spent years being psychologically hammered by an abusive partner, you start doubting not just your own judgement but your right to even have a worthwhile opinion. Logically, I knew I was being abused and bullied, but psychologically it had become so normalised I needed external affirmation. So I began Googling for answers and printed some of those most relevant to me."

Printed on 24th June 2011, 10.28am

Does your partner:
Humiliate or yell at you?
Criticise or put you down?
Blame you for their own abusive behaviour?
Have a bad and unpredictable temper?
Hurt, threaten to hurt or kill you?
Threaten to take your children away or harm them?
Threaten to commit suicide if you leave?
Destroy your belongings?
Act excessively jealous and possessive?
Control where you go or what you do?

From *http://www.helpguide.org/mental/*

In only one of these behaviours is physical violence against Victim listed, the other is against Victim's possessions. All other threats and actions, over 80% of it, relates to coercive/psychological control, threats against others and emotional abuse.

Printed on 24th June 2011, 10.28am

Economic or financial abuse: a subtle form of emotional abuse
Withholding basic necessities (including shelter)
Sabotaging your job.

From *http://www.helpguide.org/mental/*

"I'm glad I kept these printouts. They remind me of how justified I was to fight back and for how many years they made it

their purpose in life to destroy me, regardless of any cost to the children, while telling me it was my fault for making them *have* to do it. Easy to see how awful they were now but when you are in it, psychologically put down so much you are made to feel hopeless and helpless, how do you even begin an escape from your own home? I couldn't think of one that would work in practice so kept going as I had been, trying to find a way forward with them."

Printed on 24th June 2011, 10.28am

You may think that physical abuse is far worse than emotional abuse, since physical violence can send you to the hospital and leave you with scars. But, the scars of emotional abuse are very real, and they run deep. In fact, emotional abuse can be just as damaging as physical abuse – sometimes more so.

From http://www.helpguide.org/mental/

This again brings us back to the nonsense with which Women's Aid, and the government policies they seem to run, misrepresenting domestic violence as a male only crime, with only passing lip service towards all victims. Yes, there is no question there are more females than males who are seriously physically injured or killed during domestic violence but what about those 'man up and take it' female attacks that go unreported and unnoticed by a society constantly told that only females suffer domestic abuse? What about the endless emotional abuse, potentially more harmful than physical, that many face on a regular basis that goes unreported or gets laughed off if it is? And when a man does ask for help, even with supporting evidence he is the victim, how readily can the female abuser use her position as a female, often tearfully, to DARVO the situation? With the widespread mindset that the females are victims, the answer is it happens all the time. Why else are 92% of prosecutions against males when at least a third of the recorded abuse is suffered by males?

"Being on the patient panel at our local surgery, I knew we had some great doctors and made an appointment to get some advice. To be honest, although I went to this GP three or four times, I don't remember what I was told – beyond feeling relief I was listened to and that some kind of record was being made. Even before my arrest and policed mistreatment in 2008, I had doubted justice for victims, and I saw these records as part of establishing me as the victim if the need ever arose."

Abuser's 2012 Diary, written on the front page

'A problem will get heavier when the only person carrying it is you', anon

Chapter 12

Finances

"Abuser remained angry at not being able to live like royalty"

1 year before escape

"By 2012, financial abuse had become another key part of Abuser's behaviour. My well-paid undercover TV work had dried up after the 2008 recession - not because the broadcasters didn't offer funding but because the organisations we wanted to investigate weren't recruiting. As a result I branched out into mystery shopping, having the undercover equipment and skills to do it. The pay was hardly worth it so, having a clean driving licence, I joined an agency for car, van and lorry driving on a zero hours contract.

Being on zero hours and being driving, often at night, I had to ensure I slept during days in case I got called in. If I didn't get called in I didn't get paid a penny so could never afford to say no. Although I got great feedback from clients, some weeks I got a lot of work, others not much. One of the clients I ended up doing a lot of work for was a local airline, driving pilots between airports and the base. Often they were too tired to talk after long shifts but other times we would chat and my situation with Abuser began to spill out. *'I would never let someone talk to me like that'*, one said. Normally, neither would I.

All the while, despite my having effectively put my TV and film career on hold, all Abuser saw was a lack of riches and they continued to rant and belittle, including hurling their favourite brick: *'You're a fucking alcoholic loser.'* Meanwhile, they carried on shopping for designer clothes, as if they were the millionaire they felt they deserved to be."

Abuser's Diary, 29th February 2012

16.25-21.10 Birmingham – Kaunas

"Abuser was on their way to Daugavpils in Latvia, via a nearby Lithuanian airport, to bring their elderly mum over for a holiday with us."

Abuser's Diary, 2nd March 2012

Back.   Riga 17.45 – 18.20

"This was the day their mother, now a widower, arrived. Their father had died a few years earlier, while we were staying with them in Latvia - slipping in the bath and hitting his head while we slept. I was the last person to ever speak to him and wondered if he had some premonition he was going to die, as he'd asked me to help to sort out some of his possessions and gifted me with a prized set. His was the first open casket funeral I or the boys had ever seen – and hopefully the last.

Abuser's mother arrived in the UK, barely able to walk and with English no better, she was accommodated in the rear section of our living room, next to the kitchen/diner on a large sofa bed. She only planned to stay for a holiday but Abuser grew other ideas, involving a plan for pension fraud to pay for their retail therapy."

Abuser's Diary, 10th April 2012

> Kids go to granny (Victim's mum)

Abuser's SMS To Victim's Mum, 14th April 2012, 18.35

> Could you keep kids a day longer (until Monday) please? Victim keeps drinking, we are arguing non-stop and I did not manage to do everything I planned while kids are away. Abuser.

"We weren't arguing non-stop – arguing takes two voices. Abuser was simply shouting non-stop. I was working as a driver, mostly taxiing car loads of pilots between airports. If I had been drinking like Abuser said how could I have been doing this without complaint? At work the pilots considered me one of their best and most trusted drivers. Never late, always a reliable, safe smooth drive, whatever the weather or traffic conditions. I didn't want to be a driver, I wanted to go back my TV and film work but after the 2008 recession it wasn't reliable or steady and the driving paid enough to cover the bills until something else took off. Rather than appreciate this career sacrifice, Abuser remained angry at no longer being able to live like royalty."

Abuser's Diary, 15th April 2012

> London with mum?
>
> Find out if it's possible. (due to wheeled walker access)

Abuser's Diary, 10th June 2012

> Take mum back (to Latvia) or not?

"The reason Abuser didn't take their mother home was because of their money fraud idea – inspired by seeing others do the same. Their plan was to claim Pension Credits for their mother while she was staying with us and then continue to do so after they had returned to Latvia. Easy money, they thought so carried on spending."

Abuser's Diary, 14th June 2012

5 weeks before I will fly away.

Abuser's Diary, 1st July 2012

Olympic Flame at Memorial Park, 4.30pm.

"Abuser made this note in their diary about the Olympic flame to be carried though Coventry that day, but it was me who took the children to see the runner carrying it. Abuser had trashed my home office yet again and keyed my car with: *'GET BACK MY CAR YOU IDIOT',* in large letters into the passenger door, after I had borrowed theirs to go to work one night. I had begun recording them – for evidence in case the police ever got involved again. I could see it becoming more when than if."

Abuser's car was blocking Victim's so they borrowed their car to go to work for an extra shift, to escape abuse. This is what Abuser did to their car after they left.

VICTIM	So you're not letting me sleep at all before a 30-hour shift.
ABUSER	Don't care.
VICTIM	So what should I do. Quit?
ABUSER	I want you to die.
VICTIM	So you want me to quit the job?
ABUSER	I want you to die. I want you to crash and die. This is what I want. Then I will be free from you.

Abuser's Diary, 13ᵗʰ July 2012

Liverpool – Riga, 6.35 – 11.15.

"Abuser and I flew to Latvia for their niece's wedding. Granny, my mum, came up to look after them, despite Abuser still deriding me in front of her and the children. It wasn't the first time."

Abuser's Diary, 14ᵗʰ July 2012

Kaski wedding, 3.40pm.

"Kaski refers to Kasia (Kate), the niece whose wedding we had flown out to celebrate, leaving our children to be looked after by my mother. The wedding went well and, away from day to day life, Abuser was able to play the part of royalty who lived in England. They looked happy with the illusion and their ranting stopped. People even commented to them on how well behaved I was – which seemed a bit odd when they told me. It seemed they never considered my upset was a result of Abuser being abusive. Mostly, I was just glad the shouting had stopped. Abuser looked particularly happy while being the star of the wedding party, as they took the microphone from their sister and sang to the crowd."

Abuser's Diary, 15ᵗʰ July 2012

Take mum's marriage certificate.

"Abuser needed their mother's marriage certificate for their Pension Credit fraud plan. I had my first Russian sauna, complete with birch branch 'beating' then a jump into a cold lake. Was fun."

Booked for 16th July 22.20 – 22.55, Riga-Liverpool.

"16th July was when we flew back to the UK. Abuser's mum had gone to stay with Abuser's brother in nearby Leamington Spa, while my mum had stayed at our home to look after the children. Back in England, Abuser returned to 'normal'. Within days they were asking my mum to take the kids to her home in Kent again, so they could have a break. My mum agreed. The kids loved going to her place – no arguments with my stepdad, Tony, private woodland to play in and two fluffy Alsatian dogs to play with."

Chapter 13

Parasite

"I wish mum would die so we can be happy without arguments.", Alan

9 months before escape

Abuser's Diary, 6th August 2012

> Kids can go to gran. (Victim's mum)

"When granny was bringing them home on the train, Alan told her: 'I wish my Abuser would die so we could be happy without arguments.' Alan was only 7-years old at the time. How sad is that, for a 7-year-old to find his own parent such a monster to live with that prefers them to be dead? I never told Abuser he said that because they would punish him for it.

Financially, we were both working and the way we split the bills was this":

ABUSER	VICTIM
In: Wages and Child Benefit, Child Care Credits and Child Tax Credits	**In:** Self employment and Working Tax Credits
Out: 75% of rent, children's parties and occasional trips, petrol for self, some food, own mobile phone, own clothes and some of the occasional family trips abroad.	**Out:** 25% of rent, 100% gas, water, electric, home telephone, internet, both car repairs, petrol for self, some food, own mobile phone, own clothes and most of the occasional family trips abroad.

"Wanting to feel and look like royalty, Abuser was spending an ever increasing fortune on designer clothes. To the point that they ended up flat broke at the end of each month after we paid the rent. Rather than trying to budget, they blamed me for us not having more money and, conveniently 'forgetting' all the other stuff I was paying for - began accusing me of being a loser and a parasite. We both ended up borrowing too much money on credit cards. While I also took out bank loans, Abuser took out payday loans – then payday loans to cover payday loans, some at over 5000% interest. Not a typo.

To make Abuser's moods even worse, they got notification, dated 10th August 2012, that their fraudulent attempt to claim UK Pension Credits for their mother had been rejected. Abuser had been sure they would get a lump sum payment for it and had already spent money they now wouldn't get. As usual, Abuser's response was anger."

> Elizabeth's (Victim's mum's) birthday. Fuck her, kill her and hang XXXX.

"By late 2012, Abuser's spending was out of control. They had justified their spiralling debts with the back-dated Pension Credit scam they had been expecting for their elderly Latvian mother, now living with us for five months on our sofa bed. Abuser's mother had wanted to return home ages ago and didn't like the idea of any money from the British government but Abuser gave her no choice and pushed her into signing the English language documents she couldn't even understand. When the claim was rejected Abuser was left not just with the annoyance of having looked after their mum for five months but also the large, rapidly increasing debts they now couldn't pay. Their answer? To send their mother home, get angry with the chasing creditors and get even more angry with me.

The kids were seven and eight now and I could see the negative effects their abuse was having on them. Alan would keep himself on the front line, trying to calm them down, while Paul sometimes stood toe to toe with them, shouting back in defiance. No child should be faced with any of that."

> 9.45am XXXX medical centre (interpreting work)
>
> 13.15 XXXX Clinic (interpreting work)
>
> 4.00 John (Abuser's brother, their visit to him)

"The next day, Abuser began kicking off as I was preparing for another night shift. Brave Alan tried to get their attention to calm them down, while Paul stood kicking a wall in frustration. I started recording it and told them I was doing so – they didn't care. Even reminding them again, saying 'keep going' as I showed them the

Transcript: 15ᵗʰ August 2012, 6pm, Victim getting ready for work -

ABUSER	(to Victim) Prepare for kids.
ALAN	Mummy. No.
ABUSER	What mummy? What no?
PAUL	XXXX
VICTIM	XXXX
ALAN	XXXX go to park.
ABUSER	Daddy crossed the line yesterday and needs to pay for this.
ALAN	Mummy you also XXXX
ABUSER	You're either fucking out from my life or
ALAN	Mummy.
ABUSER	Stop messing XXXX
VICTIM	I'm recording.
ALAN	Mummy! Should I open the door so people can see as that's the only way to make you stop. To open the door.
ABUSER	Daddy left us. He didn't care.
VICTIM	Daddy went to work
ABUSER	I asked daddy to come to the park he said "I have my work to do because…" Blah, blah.
VICTIM	You were fine at the time.
ABUSER	No, I wasn't fine. I was before work. I was running late everywhere but I was still thinking about kids.
VICTIM	You weren't late for work.
ABUSER	You selfish fucking pig.
VICTIM	You went to John (their brother, confirmed in their diary).
ABUSER	You just think about yourself. And yourself. And yourself. And Yourself.
ALAN	Mummy. Mummy. Mummy. Mummy.
VICTIM	Keep going (showing Abuser the recorder to remind them he is recording)

ABUSER	You always think about yourself
ALAN	Mummy. Mummy. Mummy. And mummy.
ABUSER	XXXX
ALAN	Mummy. Mummy. Mummy. Mummy. Mummy. Mummy.
VICTIM	XXXX
ABUSER	Big deal. Drink cider and London debts.
ALAN	Mummy. Mummy. Mummy. Mummy.
ABUSER	And stupid (spits) debts.
ALAN	Mummy. Stop it.
ABUSER	Forget stars. I don't have money, daddy does. He can pay stars for you. He can buy you gifts. He can pay for your stars.
VICTIM	What about the gifts? Why are you saying that?
ABUSER	Oh see, daddy's saying he doesn't care.
ALAN	Mummy!
ABUSER	Oh kids just listen to this. He doesn't care. Mummy started. Mummy started.
ALAN	You don't care! Mummy......

Yes, Abuser is the mother, Victim is the father.

"In total it continued for about half an hour, Abuser's mother downstairs listening to it all – with her poor English not understanding the words, only that Abuser was ranting at Victim, in front of their distressed children. Abuser followed me outside as I got in my car to go to work, further distressing Alan with embarrassment as he could see some passers by were listening. The stars Abuser refers to were the gold reward stars the children collected for good behaviour. When they got a full sheet they got £25. When Paul said he would live with me, they ripped his sheet up in front of him."

Abuser's use of the children's happiness as weapons against Victim is totally ruthless. When they state Victim doesn't care about them, even Alan, aged just seven at the time, can be heard telling them they are the one who doesn't care. Even a child can see the truth, while the abuser refuses to.

According to Women's Aid, 61.7% of female victims in refuges had children under the age of 18. The are no refuges for abused fathers with children.

Abuser's Diary, 25th August 2012

Mama will fly to Latvia.

"Not only did the financial abuse increase, knowing I was paying all the utilities, Abuser decided to punish me by deliberately leaving on the lights and heating when they left for work. I would came home after a night shift to find literally everything on and the heating turned up to 46 degrees centigrade, the highest it could go, even on hot, sunny days. It felt like walking into Africa.

Having ruined their finances with payday loans and store card debts to support their shopping excesses, Abuser started threatening and then withholding their part of the rent, while still taking out more payday loans, getting multiple £25 bank charges every month and a parking fine they also chose to ignore, which escalated. Their entire attitude to their creditors was similar to their attitude to me - they would rage and to tell them to literally FUCK OFF! Sometimes I managed to get some bank charges withdrawn – sometimes I couldn't as they had annoyed them too much. As for the parking fine, having once worked in a call-centre dealing with such things, I told them how to get it reset. They didn't bother."

Chapter 14

Marriage Guidance Booked

"You made me to be a sadist"

8 months before escape

September 2012.

"Trying to save our marriage, I decided to go teetotal for six weeks, to see how things improved. At first Abuser was pleased, but then they started complaining about other things instead. Now I was accused of spending too much time in cafés, which I did once a day with my laptop for writing work, and then I was accused of having too much fun by going to aikido twice a week. Finally I understood. It didn't matter what I did, Abuser would always find something to complain about. As a last resort, I booked us into Relate for couple's counselling."

The following transcript, mostly Abuser's monologue, is segmented according to their momentary pauses.

Transcript: 11th September 2012, daytime -

ABUSER	And I will fucking smash your head against a wall. And I wouldn't even worry about it. As a matter of fact I'm not worried about anyone. I'm so changed person. Imagine what I would do if my mum died. You know what I'd do (spits) like this. Because I don't care about my mum. I don't care about John (their brother) and I don't care about you and I don't fucking care about anyone. This is how you changed me. You made me to be a sadist you deserve.
ABUSER	You know enough is enough. I've been raped as 18-year old girl. I've been fucking abandoned because I'm not a virgin by Tom I've been fucking tortured by you all this life by alcoholics. I had alcoholic dad. I've been very strong all my life. Very strong but believe it or not I fucking broke now. I can't recognise myself. Look at what I fucking became. Congratulations
ABUSER	Fucking bunch of sadists. Just sucking on me and sucking and sucking. And coming to me only when you need something. I'm not going to work. I'm cancelling my sessions tomorrow. I have none tomorrow. None the day after tomorrow and generally I not earning any fucking a penny. What for? All money I'll have

51

	I'm buying drugs. Maybe I'll have find some soothing. Enough of this. This isn't life. Fucking making life for you. For person who doesn't want any decency.
ABUSER	I'm having fun (mocking Victim). I'm drinking because I'm having fun. So fucking have a fun at my funeral. You selfish bastard. They're having fun. God damn you. Fuck.
VICTIM (to the recorder)	This is Abuser getting stressed about Thursday's visit to Relate, in two days.
ABUSER	Not for one, for a second believe it's because of us and you want to improve something. No. It's because if I'll divorce you in a court you want to look nice. So as if you were trying to do something and another proof since you made an effort not to drink once in your life time, and I'm underlining once in your life time, you want some kind of third party proof for this too. So other people will see how well and sober you are. 'Cause you're a fucking bastard. Deep inside you're a bastard
ABUSER	Not going to fool someone with your pretences. No fucking way. Everybody can know that you're an alcoholic. All neighbours in Northfield. All neighbours here. If you think your 3 weeks will save you you're very very delusioned.
ABUSER	Fuck you. You know what. I need my room so you can fucking move out and sleep under your table. You know we don't have family. You don't have a wife. And don't ask me for sex any more because I'm fed up from crying after this.
ABUSER	In the past I used to imagine that I'm fucking with someone else, at least it was some kind of excitement. Now I'm run out fantasies because I don't have any fantasies. I fucking don't have any fantasies. I don't love anyone including myself. This is why I'm butchering my arms non-stop. And look how they look like and I bloody will not be able to swim for rest of my life with kids. Thank you dear. Are you enjoying yourself are you? I hope you are. Don't you want to fucking drink more? And live on your payments. Go and make your useless film. Or maybe five films. Or maybe seven. Why not? Instead of building family and investing in your family he will be investing in your fucking rubbish ideas.
ABUSER	You lost your chances. Go and bloody clean streets now. £5.80 and I will be on Jobseeker's Allowance. This is the wife you fucking deserved. I hate you. And these clothes by the way is

> the clothes given by my mum and Susan. This why they're here in case you're wondering. I'm going to bloody burn them tonight. Including this (holds up a dress). This where I fucked with you for the first time. Fuck this memory forever. Don't want any of it. You know all this sentiment (spits). Not worth anything.

This is a verbal explosion of the internal internal emotions in Abuser's shadow that they have never learnt to deal with. The timing is significant. Not only can they no longer complain about Victim drinking alcohol, because they aren't, but they knows they will be raising their issues with their rages and abuse with the counsellor, meaning Abuser is likely to be challenged by someone in a position of authority. If there is one thing a narcissist hates it is being challenged, especially by someone in authority, hence the rant.

"I found it relatively easy to remain calm when Abuser was ranting - it had become almost the norm for me. Believe it or not I still felt empathy for them, this ranting partner I had fallen in love with, because despite everything they threw at me, I could see they were in pain. Even if it was pain of their own invention. I just hoped the meeting I'd booked at Relate could help us forward."

Transcript: 12ᵗʰ September 2012, early hours -

ABUSER	You know the solution? Me and kids dying in some car crash and fucking starting a life somewhere else.
VICTIM	Why do you want kids to die as well?
ABUSER	Because I believe that soul will live. And you will be left alone in this world. This will be fuck-tastic for me. It's exactly what you always wanted. You didn't want family. You didn't want any links with me. You didn't want any investment in your family. You don't give a shit about your family. All you want are your achievements and your films, films, films (spits).

"I didn't take this comment about dying in a deliberate car crash as an intention, just another sign of how stressed Abuser felt about the upcoming Relate meeting. Looking back on it now, seven years later and in my third year of therapy, I no longer feel sympathy for Abuser. Upon reflection, I think their habit of spitting, as well as their ranting, was learnt from their mother, possibly reinforced during her five-month stay at our house earlier that year."

While counselling sessions can help with 'normal' couples, when there is someone with the narcissistic personality disorder Abuser clearly seems to have, counselling has no chance of resolving the root cause of their mental unrest. While a high-level psychotherapist could potentially do so, it would only be possible if Abuser was actually willing to admit the issues are theirs and face the childhood demons in their shadow. Given their resistance to even see a counsellor, let alone their narcissistic focus of projecting their issues on others, that remains incredibly unlikely. On the plus side, they both went to the Relate counselling for weekly, Thursday sessions, with Craig.

"It didn't take long for Craig, our appointed counsellor to see I was the one who would listen to reason. Rather than struggling to deal with Abuser's behaviour, I became the one asked to compromise, as it was clear they wouldn't. Despite all evidence to the contrary, Abuser's favourite brick of 'alcoholic' was thrown at me again, as it had been by their mother against their father. I offered to drink just four cans a week, at a time of my choosing. Abuser refused, demanding I never drank anything, which I had already discovered was just a way of controlling me and that, once achieved, they simply complained about something else, so I refused too. Nothing would have been gained, except more manipulation by Abuser, if I had said yes."

Chapter 15

Text War

"You piece of crap, fucking bastard", Abuser.

7 months before escape

"With me driving at night and communication issues during the day, our communication method became text messages."

Victim's SMS, 04/10/2012, Thu, 12.32

Coming to relate?

"Abuser didn't reply but we had the marriage-guidance meeting I'd booked and I went to my long distance driving work."

Victim's SMS, 04/10/2012, Thu, 21.21

Not over hsbc limit.

Abuser's SMS, 04/10/2012, Thu, 22.32

Ok. Vgood luck with your work.

Victim's SMS 05/10/2012 Fri, 01.04

Thanks. Lots of roadworks and diversions and bad weather. Still wondering about relate next week.

"Once home after work, I slept for a bit then went to a café to do some writing."

Victim's SMS 05/10/2012 Fri, 15.56

Can you collect kids?

16.11

Not heard back so walking to collect them. Paid council tax and for relate.

16.53

We are all at home.

"Abuser came home and began a new nightmare, despite the

apparent pleasantness earlier, the cause of which will become clear in the following SMS exchange after I began another night shift."

Consider the contradiction of the following email when reading the rest of the 2012 SMSes:

Abuser's email, 10th January 2020, 11.24

...did not want divorce yet if Victims schizophrenia took over them and their behaviour- its not my responsibility and never will be...

Bad memory, denial or attempt to manipulate the truth? Either way, the Abuser's SMSes continued:

Abuser's SMS, 5/10/2012. 20.25

Want divorce as can't be humiliated any more by an alcoholic like you.

20.26

Wish you were dead or vanished for ever somewhere.

20.26

You will pay for insulting me in front of yarka (their nephew) and even if will go to ferrari tomorrow it will be for one reason: to embarrass you in front of mark (my friend) and damien (my brother).

Victims SMS reply, 20.35

You denied me sleep before night shift. Was already paying before your stupid comment which triggered my insult and just paid £7 for coffee and choc to keep awake without sleep. Say what crap you like to anyone who knows me – they will know it is exactly that.

Abuser's SMS response, 20.42

You can't control your aggressive attacks but expect me to control my panic attacks. You fucking idiot. Leaving keys in the door and you can sleep in the car or waste your life as you wish. Hate you for your abusive character.

Abuser is projecting their behaviours on Victim.

56

20.42

You are a liar, you can't sleep anyway. Every time I approached you upstairs you were playing on your phone. Be angry with yourself and your alcohol damaged brain instead.

Victim's SMS reply, 20.53

I played phone game for 5 mins only to relax. You only know because you came to disturb me. You were on your phone for almost and hour!!!!!

"They had been chatting loudly, deliberately ruining my sleep before my night shift."

Abuser's response, 21.43

So what? My sister needed my help. Yarka came as he needed my help. You came to the kitchen calling me a fucking bitch. Shall I report you to police?

21.44

Not planning to forgive you. The only fucking bitch I know is your mum.

Victim's SMS reply, 21.49

So when you swear it is ok. And stop lying. Your sister didn't need your help about the bank complaint that second. Banks have been closed for hours.

Abuser's SMS response, 22.16

I am tired of your aggressiveness.

You would not need to work nights if you had an ability to plan ahead and chose boring but stable career instead of no career and unjustified ambitions. Family suffers more than you as a result of your stupidness.

Here we have passive aggressive, *'you would not need to work nights if you planned ahead'*, mixed with further projecting - it was Abuser's own career that was not as they wanted and they were the aggressive one, not Victim.

Victim's reply, 22.30

Am totally placid by nature

Like throwing chairs in cieszyn. Throwing bottle at wall when I was holding 2-week old Paul? You are a coward. Running away from relate and then poisoning me with your aggression at home so yarka and kids can admire your selfishness.

"In Cieszyn, the Polish town we had first lived in together, Abuser had thrown chairs and bottles, smashed a window with a mug aimed at my head and trashed my home office stuff. In England, after marriage, they continued trashing my home office and throwing things, often at me."

You have to go back 8 and 10 years to give examples? Wow. How awful I am...

You threw bottles at me. Am driving now. Night. Raining hard. Deliberately denied sleep by you and 500km to go. No need to wish me to crash any more as you have already done the preparation. Dziwka (bitch).

Stuck in traffic. Lucky me.

After you are unreasonable at next relate meeting lets sit in a cafe and fill out divorce papers together. Have printed them off.

Fill out papers yourself and remember I am not a dziwka (bitch) but you are definitely a loser alcoholic and please continue losing without me. Bye.

If someone you wanted to really divorce asked you to help fill out the divorce papers, would you not be keen to do so? The point I am making is Abuser did not actually want a divorce, just the threat of it as a control mechanism against Victim. The only time abusers want to lose their punchbags is when they can get something else by doing so. If Victim left this supposed 'parasite' they would no longer be paying bills/rent, looking after the children or fixing their car and, worst of all, they might find someone kind and be happy without them; effectively demonstrating that Abuser is the issue not Victim. A narcissist's fragile ego would never stand this. If, on the other hand,

58

Victim crashed and died at work, not only would Abuser's ego be intact but they could also claim the inheritance and sympathy for their loss. Silently knowing they had killed through sleep deprivation.

Abuser next SMS: 00.48

And nobody denied your sleep. Its not normal to expect your family to be quiet in the evening. You also were treating me much worse when I was pregnant. How about my needs of rest, security and stability. Did you ever even think about it? I bet never. You are growing in your selfishness higher and higher. Guess what? I don't care about you at all. You lost me for ever so continue to invest in your rubbish projects instead of family.

00.54

I might be from the shouty family but yours is far worse as it consists of silent sadists. No surprise that you are one of them. Go and join your nasty sisters and conditionally loving mum and stop poisoning me with your natural rudeness so well hidden by your stupid charm when you feel guilty...

01.04

Now in your language: I will not need you, you piece of crap fucking bastard. Feel at home?

"This was from someone refusing to fill out divorce papers."

01.10

Why don't you just move out like other normal men? Even Tony had more guts and morals than you. His wife betrayed him but he still left her the whole house. We don't have anything to divide and kids are not dividable. You can have them 3-4 days per week or see them whenever you want. Not a problem for me. Just leave me alone and stop torturing me with your endless problems, drinking and frustration.

And here we have it. Abuser doesn't want divorce, just Victim kicked about like a slave, while still legally roped to them and gifting them their possessions.

01.44

If you usually come back from work about 6am. Don't tell me that sleeping until 1 or 2 is not enough you greedy bastard. You will never be sleeping in the evening in this house. Its my final rule. Perhaps it will speed up your moving out process.

01.48

I sleep on average less than you. Stop wasting your time playing games non-stop. How you even dare to blame anyone for your own stupidness? Forget earplugs. Very angry. So angry with you that would love to see you joining your father (deceased) in a useless fathers parade.

01.49

Go to ferrari yourself. Taking kids somewhere else

01.52

Fed up with your rudeness. Fed up for real. Your mum will be getting abuse from me for the rest of her life. She deserved the crucifixion that fucking whore who kicked out my son. And you are part of her so nothing nice can be expected. Hate you both.

01.54

And its nothing to do with Tony. He can be justified as were technically strangers to him while your mum is a sadistical bitch who should be eaten by her dogs to death.

"Now in a service station, I was finally able to reply to their monologue."

Victim's SMS reply, 01.54

Go to direct gov website. Download divorce papers and fill out your parts.

01.57

NOW please. And stop sending abuse. Just got to Lancaster hour late because of shit traffic and all this shit from you too is as pointless as expecting anything reasonable from you. Direct gov will come up in google search. Now FUCK OFF! Thanks.

Abuser's SMS response, 01.58

You fucking idiot crap alcoholic move out first. its in your todays style. Pleased? Without seeing you for some time I might recover from unhappiness you give me and then will be able to negotiate better deal in court.

Again, Abuser wants everything on their terms. Victim made to suffer threats of divorce court, while Abuser repeatedly refuses divorce proceedings.

> You started abuses in this family and its your fault kids are not ready for tomorrows party and your fault I can't sleep and your fault everything? Hope you are enjoying. Don't care about you. Just dont.

02.02

> I wish I never see you again but god does not love me that much recently.

Victim's SMS reply, 02.32

> I am at work. Driving. Zero alcohol. Zero running away. Zero crap from me just constant abuse from you. Time will not stop you from being abusive or aggressive. It is who you are and I can't take it any more. And you've already slept more than me – which is why I have had to stop for coffee.

Abuser's SMS response, 02.36

> I cant fall asleep only because you chose to call me a fucking bitch for nothing in front of yarka and ruin everything. I want a revenge so going to put you down in front of everyone tomorrow.

Revenge, one of a narcissist's favourite actions against anyone that dares defy them.

02.37

> Your fault you fucking idiot.

A narcissistic favourite: projecting, telling those they abuse it is their fault.

"I tried calling them to talk but they refused to pick up their phone. Infuriating."

Victim's SMS reply, 02.37

> Fucking coward too chicken to talk!!!!!!

Abuser's SMS response, 03.19

> No keys in the door by the way and still cant sleep because of you.

Apparently afraid of having been too terrible and losing their punchbag again, Abuser invites Victim back home, letting them know they are not locked out this time.

I left for work 8 hours ago. Had to stop for next coffee and done nothing but get abuse from you last 9 hours – with your excuse I was rude when you refused to let me sleep.

Interestingly, Abuser doesn't retaliate or abuse Victim for this defiant reply. They must have been afraid they really could lose them.

Abuser's Diary, 6ᵗʰ October 2012

Victim's Ferrari.

"My brother had bought me a Ferrari driving day gift and on this day he came to our house for us all to drive to Silverstone, for me to drive the three laps in a Ferrari 360. As I drove us there, Abuser made the open announcement: *'I'm only coming to see you crash'*, among other such pleasantries. I didn't crash and had a brilliant time, not sure my brother or friend Dan did. Think they were taken aback by Abuser's endless criticisms and hateful wishes. For me it was just Abuser, my abusive spouse, as normal and during my next night shift the SMS abuse resumed too."

Abuser's SMS, 8/10/2012, 02.36

Planning to smoke everyday now.

If you don't like it – its purely your own problem. Will forget about offline mode (mobile phone flight mode) too. Let radiation live! You were disrespecting my values for ages its my turn to flush yours down the toilet now.

Victim, Abuser's punchbag, had gone back home and they feel they can get away with abusing them again. Knowing Victim hates cigarettes because their dad died from smoking, they use smoking as a new tool for torture and again use their love for the children as a weapon against them. Abuser also stubbed out cigarettes on their head and face in front of the children.

So you want our kids to be senile by the age of 50. Smoke 500 a day but outside the house, or do you want the kids crying with breathing conditions?

And stop trying to bully me. Good night

"I was so fed up I decided to sleep in my car, again, around a corner - just 100 yards from our home."

Abuser's SMS response, 12.37

Are you not at home yet?

Abuser is now worried they have lost their punchbag.

Victim's reply, 12.39

What home? Land of shouting queen wannabee and controller of all thoughts and aims forever.

Abuser's SMS, 12.39

You were drinking cause you wanted our kids to become alcoholics and losers? The same logic as with smoking, but it took you 10 years to understand it.

12.42

Fine by me. And yes I am a queen, queen of my damaged life to which you lost access.

Abuser is attacking, pretending they don't care if they have lost them now.

13.33

At home. Probably got flu.

And now Abuser is feeling sorry for themself and wanting sympathy, trying to pull Victim back within their grasp.

13.42

And now I feel more miserable than you.

If only narcissists knew how to feel sorry for anyone but themselves.

Victim's SMS, 15.01

Helping yarka (Abuser's nephew who lived in nearby Leamington Spa) with forms jutro (tomorrow). No bullying from you accepted.

I never accepted your drinking but you wont respect this. Why should I let you make rules if you did not earn this position?

Is Victim demanding Abuser does not bully them something unreasonable?

19.09

Don't care if you are coming home or not. Feel nice without you though.

The reply of a petulant child.

Victim's SMS, 19.09

Rubbish bins need to go out.

Abuser's SMS, 19.43

Ok. Going to asda now as tomorrow kids go to church with harvest gifts.

19.44

Its painful for me to live with atheist like you. Its not school but parents who should initiate visits to church and the rest.

19.45

I have 0 spiritual support on the top of having zero of intellectual and psychological. It's impossible to be happy with somebody who chose alcohol over me and laughs at my values. Pleased you are not here.

Victim's SMS, 19.46

Last time we went to church you came home with demon rage and hurt alan by throwing a cola bottle. Zero alcohol. Just you and holy church.

19.47

Easy to feel good in a 'free hotel'. Yarka coming for help jutro (tomorrow).

19.49

Rent is yours not mine this month.

Fine, as long as you will leave the property. I don't want you. Feel so nice without you that completely cant understand why I was so stupid for so many years to suffer living with you in hope that one day you will marry me (we were married), will come to your senses and will start living family life. Your request for me to pay rent is another proof that you are not capable to support your family. Ask Matthew if Susan pays mortgage. You are a miserable little man.

Victim's SMS, 20.05

Jestem dobre (I am good).

"Abuser had refused to follow my guidance on how to reset their parking fine, leaving it to escalate, so I had done it for them."

20.07

Don't forget your parking ticket. I won't be able to get it reset again.

Abuser's SMS, 20.15

Thanks. Will be paid tomorrow instead of kids dinners. Unless I will take out another loan. You earned more than me last month yet did not contribute a penny towards kids clothes, dinners, after school care, stagecoach or even meat from yarka. My £120 by some unexplained miracle should be enough for everything including after-school care, food, parking, petrol and stagecoach. Since I have an urge for independence and unsupportive husband I am pushed to find money where ever.

Victim's SMS, 20.21

Taking 1500% loans is not finding money it is throwing money in the toilet. Your £120 (Child Tax Credits on top of their wages) is every week and totals £6000 a year, £3000 more than after school care+dinners+stagecoach+kids clothes+trips. Why the hell should kids money pay for your parking and petrol??????

20.37

Will cancel all direct debits too. Gas and electric and phone are free for you anyway. Have job interview outside Coventry next Thursday.

Abuser's SMS, 20.38

Why all my pay should pay for rent. You owe banks more than me and wasted a fortune on your london project, hotels equipment. And you live in cuckoo land not knowing how much kids clothes cost and not ever buying a single curtain or thing for the house.

> Good for us. Don't worry – I will manage somehow. Nothing can be worse than living with an alcoholic-sadist.

Victim's SMS, 20.41

> Kids clothes do not cost the £3000 a year you have extra from government after care, dinners and stage school. I do worry as only an idiot takes loans for 1500%.

Abuser's SMS, 20.56

> Even if I am an idiot its not greater than yours. If you want to be jealous, be jealous not about how much it is spent on kids, and almost everything is, but how much your friends from the same university are earning which eliminates the need to torture their wives for money. Trips are paid for you, restaurants, clothes and furniture – cant stop regretting ever paying for you. Even that 40 towards your coat, would you pay 40 for mine?

Again Abuser points out their displeasure is money based and, as not unusual for a narcissist, complains about the £40 towards the coat they wanted Victim to buy, to look more upmarket like them. In both cases it is about their wants and jealousy of others. One way forward would have been to work together to help improve their finances, instead Abuser is focused on financial destruction, while blaming Victim for their woes.

Victim's SMS, 20.57

> The 3000 extra from government covers all this.

20.58

> You personally pay for none of it.

Abuser's SMS, 21.14

> What do you spend £20 from the government? I suggest you will start to pay for dinners. If we are divorcing I don't want to waste my time on talking to you any more. Bye.

Challenges about their actions are something narcissists really can't deal with and, consequently, push them away – usually by belittling the challenger or shouting them down (a defence mechanism).

Transcript 8th October 2012, Victim leaving for night shift

| Abuser | Don't argue, just fuck out. (*Full transcript not yet written*) |

"After this rant, when I finished my night shift, thankfully a short one, I didn't even bother going home. Just parked up round the corner from the house and readied myself to sleep in my car – again. With car keys in the boot, I secretly rebelled with a bottle of wine and got a text from an ill friend in Poland, someone I'd known longer than Abuser. *'Can you visit me?'*, Agata asked. Given Abuser's parting words and relentless rants, with me again having to sleep in my car, I thought *'fuck it, why not?'* and booked the flights there and then. Agata was pleased and so was I. Feeling liberated I sent a text to Abuser."

Victim's SMS, 23.14

Have job interview wednesday next week and away until sunday pm. Perfect for you who hates me.

23.31

Bully, fuck you! I have the interview you said I wouldn't get. I am worth more than your lies.

Abuser's SMS, 9/10/2012, Tue, 04.45

I have never said you will not get an interview. Fuck you too then and goodnight.

04.45

And stop bullying me with your unintelligent rudeness. Don't want you or your money so stop putting your nose in my finances. Its none of your business now. I am not asking you after all how much you wasted on hotels, coffees and your crap equipment.

Out of all Abuser's endless rants and criticisms, I find it interesting how they repeatedly call Victim an alcoholic, while they are mostly drinking just coffee as working as a driver. Abuser also makes no complaint of the large amounts of money they would be spending on alcohol if actually an alcoholic.

Instead, the money moans are about the cheap hotels, needed to get actual sleep, and the extra coffees needed to avoid falling asleep at the wheel; both due to Abuser's refusal to let them sleep in their house. Money that would otherwise be spent on the family. With them both working, their combined income is sufficient for a good life together. Or at least it would be were it not for all the payday loans and money lost via Abuser's retail therapy and Victim's hotel and extra café spends to stay alive.

Chapter 16

Logging Abuse

Jekyll & Hyde in nature

"Despite Abuser's 2010 conclusion of having mental health issues, by 2012 they was firmly denying any - though still complained of a burning in their head, blaming it on me for the accidental door-frame 'bump' two years earlier. They still refused to see a doctor. Didn't want to resolve anything. Just clung to recycling their list of accusations and endlessly hurling them at me, tearfully as they raged. The tears still made me feel sorry for them being so upset – a natural reaction when your partner is upset. At the time I believed the tears were real."

The typical psychology of someone with a narcissist personality disorder, as Abuser clearly has, is to only consider themselves - while projecting their internal upset on their chosen target – usually their primary victim - and can literally cry on tap. They can truly be upset, from deeply buried hurt, but their egos are too fragile to face it. Too fragile to ever admit they are the ones who need fixing. Too fragile to admit to doing any wrong or harming those they externalise their pain on to.

If a narcissist is shouting at you, just imagine they are shouting at a mirror, for everything they say against you is actually what is coming from them. Hate, cruelty, selfishness, non-caring, etc, etc... Many of their designated victims try to help or at least appease them, believing they can be reasoned with and helped to find some resolution or happiness. This is like expecting reason or mercy from a guillotine, it is never going to happen. As with psychopaths and sociopaths, narcissists feel zero empathy and zero guilt for they, in their one-way blame minds, can never feel at fault.

"Becoming ever more desperate and exhausted, I began looking for help and solutions everywhere I could think of. Looking back I think I was mad to even try but also proud of myself for trying so hard in what I now know was a hopeless situation. I did some more research on bullying and below are some key points related to my situation."

Victim printed this off 10/10/2012, at 15.54

Bullying is not a gender issue. Bullies are manipulative people (especially female bullies).

"Bullying is not a gender issue. Bullies are manipulative people (especially female bullies)"

Very well said **bullyonline.org.** Wonder how Women's Aid would respond to that?

"Despite having affirmed I was actually being bullied and not just feeling sorry for myself, I still sought positive solutions. Despite losing hope Abuser could be reasoned with, I continued booking the marriage guidance counselling at Relate, which Abuser, being Abuser, had also been using against me. Calling it my show of pretending to do something something but we still went anyway. What happened next became *'Sod's law'*, considering the timing of my impending flight to see Agata. Abuser became almost pleasant. Stopped ranting and telling me to fuck off from their life.

Was it thanks to the counselling or my pending interview for a better paid job? Either way, it made me feel guilty about going to Kraków, to the point that I considered scrapping the tickets all together. Not because the trip itself was anything wrong nor my intentions – it was just to visit to a friend with cancer - it was feeling bad because deceit was so alien to me. Why didn't I scrap the flights? It came down to this. I reminded myself had made the booking when sleeping in the back of my car, after again being told to fuck off out of Abuser's life and when telling them I was going away for a few days they told me to go for longer. I also didn't believe Abuser's pleasantness would last. Believed it could end at any time, on a whim, and I'd have let down my friend and wasted the flights for nothing.

70

Continuing my lie of being sent away for training after the interview, I took the flight to Kraków - feeling ever more guilty as Abuser was still being nice when I left. Why couldn't they have been nice earlier?"

So why was Abuser being nice now? Was it, as Victim wondered, the thought of them getting a better paid job, earning enough money to support their royalty lifestyle, or was it the fear that, if they remained horrible, with the new job Victim would have the opportunity to meet and go off with someone else? To go and do what they had been repeatedly demanding and actually get a divorce? Actually escape? Who would be Abuser's punchbag then?

Chapter 17

Affair?

"They fucked another XXXX!", Abuser

As mentioned, abusive people tend to have deep damage inside, which they fail to deal with. Their inner pain still needs some kind of outlet and, not dealing accepting it as their issue, they externalise it onto others. As a child, Abuser couldn't escape or control their raging parents so, too fragile and ashamed to go for personal therapy, they raged their issues on others, to control them instead. Victim, was the easiest target to attack.

"In Kraków, I eventually stopped feeling bad for lying to Abuser and wishing we had gone there together, for I was spending three brilliant days with Agata, rediscovering shout-free normality. Despite the illness, Agata was cheerful, friendly, calm and didn't complain or get angry over nothing – they were simply grateful for the visit and support.

Not being a natural liar, I wasn't very good at it and, naturally, Abuser found out. At the time there was a big phone network issue in Kraków and my texts to Abuser weren't getting through so they called me. Due to the network issue, it went straight to voicemail – in Polish. Clearly I was not on a UK training course."

Abuser's SMS, 18/10/2012, Thu, 21.57

Can you send me an address of the place you are staying? I don't even roughly know where you are. For some reason a Polish-speaking machine answered when I tried calling you an hour ago. Sleep well.

Victim's SMS, 23.26

I'm in Krakow. Been chosen to be sent here because of Polish experience. Nice to be here again but so many fukking tourists. My phone didn't ring when you called – just got an sms about a missed call. Dobra noc (good night). Xx

Abuser's SMS, 19/10/2012 Fri, 08.49

Its what I thought.

16.26

Since I was kept in the dark regarding your trip don't expect me to be honest with you. My life and my kids belong to me. You can stay in Krakow for good.

Victim's SMS, 16.27

Thanks for support.

Abuser's SMS, 23.42

If you ever explained what I suppose to support it would be different. Was it so difficult to inform me on current bases? Did I need to discover by chance that you are in Poland? You abused my trust and I feel stupid for worrying about you since wednesday. Don't want to see you and don't care what you are doing. Don't also ask me what I will be doing in Banbury tomorrow night.

23.42

Its not a first time you put me in depressive state. I wish I never married you.

Victim's SMS, 23.44

Komorka (mobile) network shit. I sleep alone. Be a dziwka if you choose to be. Dobra noc (good night).

Victim's SMS, 20/10/2012 Sat, 06.04

Multiple tumours in Agata. Sorry if hurt you. Was asked to visit day slept in car after you told me to fuck off and die. I sleep on sofa bed.

Abuser's Diary, 20th October 2012

9 years ago! you came to Coventry. 9 years ago! You came to Coventry!

"It wasn't my plan to be away for this anniversary and it wasn't something we celebrated. It's just the way it happened."

Abuser's SMS, 21/10/2012, Sun, 08.51, picked up at Kraków airport

Its 3am and I can't sleep. You hurt me so much...

08.51

Will do everything to remove myself and kids from your life. You don't care about them. You will find out as the last where and how.

08.51

Started to pack your things. Give me Agata's address and will send all your stuff to Poland. Should arrive within 5-7 days.

08.53

You are not trustworthy to me any more I was worried for you – you did not care about me and kids. And don't call me a dziwka as you are the biggest slut here.

08.54

You still did not explain anything? You think that vanishing like this will improve our marriage? Your birthday falls on half term and I was considering taking us somewhere. Krakow was one of the options as I want to see Gosia and Janusz who both live there. Now its obviously very bitter topic thanks to your sneakiness. Better for us if you stay in Krakow for longer as I am not prepared to face you without wanting to hurt you just as u hurt me.

08.54

I don't believe that someone like you, who did not give a monkey about the pain they caused to the XXXX of their children, including you beating me against the wall and not caring when I was in pain on many occasions, can be supportive to cancer suffers too. Stop this bullshits – you don't have a heart.

08.54

I hope you are pissing yourself with booze appropriately. I started smoking out of stress you are causing. Well done! Do you know any other selfish effective ways to destroy kids happiness?

08.54

I don't wish my children to be shown by you how to drink and how to disrespect in every respect. Oh god, will say it again: Czarek was so right to warn me against you back in 2001.

08.54

Happy 9th anniversary of us being kicked out from your mum's life. Thanks for support from you regarding this matter.

> Difference between us is that I was hurting you with words only – you doing it a nasty deeds.

This was blatantly untrue. Although Victim didn't know it then, long before Krakow happened, Abuser had paid a private detective to find their intended lover, 'W'.

"My time with Agata was such a contrast to life with Abuser. Such an awakening that, as we ate breakfast at the airport for my flight home, now having a good phone network, I finally picked up the stream of abusive messages, and found myself not wanting to leave. Abuser's messages affirmed the kind of person I would be going back to. What for? I began thinking of not going. Of staying and getting another English teaching job in Poland and staying there."

While Victim was away, Abuser had also been smashing their things, including their office and car. As for Abuser's claim they attacked with 'just words', even if just words when psychologically abusive they can actually do more harm than physical violence. Perhaps the only reason Abuser is so adamant Victim has cheated is because this is exactly what they had been trying to do (maybe had done) and exactly what they would have done in their place. Why else would one of their first reactions be a return to Banbury? To 'W's location.

"What brought me back to the UK was not missing Abuser, for I didn't at all, or any material things. It was simply the very same thing that had kept me with Abuser in the first place, parenthood. Our kids. I had always determined I would be a good, hands-on parent and they didn't deserve to be left alone with that monster."

Children are a massive hook for victims of abuse. It is not just a question of how to support themselves if they run off with the children. For many victims there is the risk of the children being given to the abuser, who would inevitably turn them into abusers or victims themselves.

Victim's SMS, 08.56

> I hope my reaction is kinder than yours if you ever have a friend with cancer.

"After writing this, I boarded the plane and flew 'home'. Landing at Liverpool airport, I picked up an SMS from Abuser, in Russian. Couldn't understand what it said but guessed it was nothing nice. Now I was really angry too. I didn't want to be there or deserve the

75

way Abuser treated me.”

Abuser's SMS, 13.04

> This SMS has some belittling abuse in Russian, which Google translate seems unable to fully comprehend.

Victim's SMS, 13.15

> I booked the flights when forced to sleep in my car! Your fault!!!!

14.01

> Krakow komorka (mobile) network was shit. Only started getting smses at the airport. Horrible.

16.26

> And sorry for not telling you first that was actually going to poland. Felt stuck in the stupid situation.

“When I got back to Coventry, I found myself walking home with resigned dread...”

Narcissists have a deep need to have everything their way. The more a narcissist the more this need. When someone has not just narcissistic tendencies but a narcissistic disorder, where the trait is so strong it disorders their life, they demand everything their way or consider it the wrong way, regardless of how impossible or unreasonable their demand may be.

Less than two weeks earlier, Abuser had been openly trying to kill Victim through sleep deprivation before their long-distance night shifts and demanding divorce but now, after a short stay with a friend they knew was seriously ill, Abuser's ego feels bruised. Victim has dared to do what they had been demanding, believing they never would. Control broken, Abuser is desperate to re-establish control and, by accusing Victim of an affair, feels every reason and excuse to let rip.

“Knowing Abuser, I could guess what kind of reception I would get at home so began video recording on my phone as approached the house. The front bay window had a massive banner saying 'My XXXX is a cheat' and, in the front garden, the desk and equipment from my home office. None of their child-tantrum abuse surprised me any more. The children greeted me, looking worried as I opened the door: *'XXXX put your things in the garden'*, they told me. *'I know.'*, I replied. Abuser heard me come in and came downstairs to begin their rant.”

76

Abuser's banner in the front window. October 2012.

"Kiddies! Daddy put his pee pee in another woman's pee pee!" October 2012.

"They never cared whether the children were present - in fact they often tried to involve them, trying to get them on their side. On this occasion, after forcing me to get on my knees to apologise, for something I hadn't done, Abuser spat in my face, saying *"Doesn't count because I forced you."* *"I tried kiddies.",* I said to our poor witnesses."

Chapter 18

Hell Anew

"I couldn't live like this any more"

While victims can lose themselves, in the normalised day to day routine of home-life abuse, if you take them out of that environment, away from their abuser, awakenings can begin.

"Resigned to being back home, I simply began carrying my office stuff and other belongings back inside. Abuser was ranting at me in bursts – escalating their rage for, once again, I refused to rage back. They began demanding Agata's phone number, which I refused to give – a defiance that they shouted about too. It didn't make any difference. It was one thing for me to get ranted at, for I had married them, but quite another for a friend to – especially an ill friend. Besides, nothing had happened between me and Agata except close friendship. Nothing sexual at all but Abuser refused to accept this. Listening to Abuser's accusations, they were so loud it was impossible not to, seven-year-old Alan looked up at me in earnest and asked: *'Did you put your pee pee in another woman's pee pee?'* 'No, munchkin.', I told him. Unlike Abuser I was not the cheating type."

If someone believes their partner has cheated, unless there is a history of them cheating, the chances are it is a projection. A sign that, under such circumstances they would have cheated and could well have already cheated. In other words, the accuser is often the one most likely to be a cheat.

"I was still recording it all on my phone, as Abuser ranted their accusations in my face and the kids stood below their line of sight – Paul was dancing about mocking them, while Alan looked on, perplexed by the whole thing. Sadly, they had become used to this kind of aggression from them.

After some time, Abuser announced they wouldn't stop unless I went on my knees and begged for forgiveness. As cringe worthy as it sounds, I did so. I got on my knees in front of them and said: *'I'm sorry, please forgive me. But I promise I didn't cheat on you.'* Abuser's response? They spat in my face and said: *'It doesn't count. You only did it because I made you.'* They didn't want a solution - just another way to put me down."

79

The entire narcissistic process is, by its very nature, a selfish one. It doesn't matter what Victim does here, Abuser will not stop their rant until they feel satiated by punishing them. Accusing them of having an affair outranks even calling them an alcoholic - in terms of a put down and sympathy grabber from others. Why would Abuser possibly want to end such a put down without having milked it for as long as possible?

"After more of their ranting, I got fed up of being a verbal punchbag and decided to try shouting back. Now I got in their face and shouted just as loudly that I hadn't had an affair and had only gone as they had been telling me to fuck off and making me sleep in my car. Abuser paused, a little taken aback by me actually shouting back for once. Then took a breath and carried on shouting as before. For me that said everything, that they had no interest in resolving anything, and I gave up even trying. Just began sorting things around the house, no longer paying attention.

Several hours later, when Abuser's blasting had waned, I went for a walk to get some air. Knowing I couldn't go back to living like this, I found myself looking in a local shop window, at adverts for places to rent. I took down the number for a room in a nearby street and sent a text there and then."

Victim's SMS, 21Oct 2012, 20.08

Hi. Saw a room ad in Devlin's (newsagent). Can I ask if still available....?

"Their reply came within minutes, confirming it was and we agreed a viewing for 7pm the following day. Only with this escape plan made did I feel ready to go 'home'. After being reminded of normality in Kraków, I was awake to just how abnormal life with Abuser was and no longer wanted to be there. How can you want to be with someone who openly wants you dead and is doing everything in their power to destroy you?"

Chapter 19

Kill

"I'll kill kids. I'll kill you. I'll kill your mum. I'll kill myself", Abuser

22nd October

"I remember it was a Monday, the day after returning from Kraków. It was about 4pm. I had collected the kids from school and was cooking dinner when Abuser came home. They were pleasant at first, calling hello to everyone but getting no response from the kids upstairs playing, they shouted hello louder to get a response – they had been too engrossed in disagreeing about a game to reply the first time. Then Abuser came to me, began saying how bad an influence our arguments were on the kids and promptly began one. By argument I mean another ranting monologue, which I was recording."

People with personality disorders tend to have minds in constant unrest. With narcissists the unrest causes an inability to feel happy, for the unhappiness inside is never resolved - projecting this against others. Blaming any flaws or events that can possibly be blamed for their upset - regardless of how long ago any such event was or anything they themselves might have done to cause it.

I'll say it again, if a narcissist calls you anything nasty or aggressive, simply imagine they are saying it into a mirror. In psychological terms they are. It can never make them feel better for long as it is not actually tackling their issues, which remain unchanged. So they simply keep on projecting, more and more as their vicious cycle of trying to feel better vanishes into failure again so they try again, harder this time.

Cycles of Abuse

Devout narcissists, similarly with psychopaths and sociopaths, feel no empathy for those they hurt and remain entirely focused on themselves, while telling you it is your fault. Attacking you to deflect from their inner pains, as if you are the cause, they find no lasting satisfaction as they are not dealing with the true cause: themselves. As with a growing addiction, they need bigger and bigger hits to gain their fleeting satisfaction

Physical abusers may start with a slap, then a harder slap, then a slight punch, then a harder punch, then harder punches... Psychological abusers might start with a bit of a complaint, then a put down, then a bigger put down with a bit of a rant, then more rants and more put downs, longer and harder...

These cycles will never end for there can be no issue resolution unless the issue itself is being dealt with, and they are attacking you specifically to avoid dealing with it. Abusing you is their subconscious idea of medicine and they will continue using you for this for as long as they can. You can't change someone who refuses to accept they need to change, even if they say they do. In most cases, saying they will is just a clawback, to get you, their 'medicine', back within grasp if you have escaped them.

Such self-medication for any abuser - domestic, alcohol or drug – is all equally pointless. The biggest difference with domestic abuse is they are consuming you, your life and well-being and that of any children you may have.

"The kids came into the kitchen, arguing over whose fizzy drink was whose, with Abuser watching their conflict and sighing at how it was our fault for arguing in front of them. It made them focus on the negative things between us and a new rant began. Knowing I had a viewing for the room in a couple of hours, I let it wash over me, as much as I could. Abuser, seeing me not getting wound up, decided to try harder and got worse.

In reality, it didn't actually matter how I responded, they would always get worse, in the same way they would always start from nothing but what ever was going on in their head. It had taken me years to realise it but, with Abuser, reason was impossible. Why? Because you can't reason with an unreasonable person."

This is a profound part of a narcissistic personality disorder. They do not want conflict resolution, they only want to harm and hurt because they can't face the harm and hurt inside themselves. 'Reasons' are just excuses and any 'reason' they can think of will do. Where does their actual hurt come from? Sadly, typically from pre-birth to two years old. This is a crucial period in both brain development and the ability to handle the stress hormone cortisol. Studies of Romanian orphans have indicated that what happens in this very earlier period of life, impacts the brain's ability to handle stress for life.

In this sense, you could argue such people are innocent of this mental issue inflicted on them as babies. On the other hand, many unhappy children choose not to repeat the cycle but to become adults behaving the exact opposite. Abuser's behaviour demonstrates they are one of the former.

"As much as the children were used to their rants, it still affected them. By accident, Abuser hit Paul yet was so blinded by self-increasing rage they ignored his protests until he resorted to shouting at them to make them listen. When they finally heard

him, they blamed it on me for making them angry. All I had been doing was cooking the family dinner. I couldn't wait to move out – that very day if possible."

Blameless is a word that describes narcissists views of themselves very well. Ever watched a documentary where a convicted murderer is talking about their victim, claiming they are innocent, despite irrefutable evidence they are not? At the same time expressing zero sorrow for their victim, only for themselves? It means a narcissist, sociopath or psychopath is talking. And they can lie so convincingly that, if you didn't know the evidence against them or the signs to look for, you could actually believe them. If they repeat their lies of innocence often enough, they may even believe them themselves.

"Abuser hadn't been home for long and had already worked themself into a frenzy. Then they upped the stakes."

Transcript: 22nd October 2012, afternoon in the kitchen -

ABUSER	You know, I'll kill kids. I'll kill you. I'll kill your mum. I'll kill myself.
VICTIM	Say that again.
ABUSER	I won't.
VICTIM	You just said you'll kill the kids?
ABUSER	I'll kill everyone.
VICTIM	You'll kill your own kids?
ABUSER	You too and myself.
VICTIM	I don't care about me. You'll kill the kids?
ABUSER	I'll kill your mum first... so she'll die in agony.
CHILD	XXXX what are you doing? What are you saying? What is wrong with you guys?

"In the past I had 'dealt' with their abuse by escaping the house for peace, even spending nights sleeping in my car or a local hotel less than a mile from home. Without me there, as a verbal punchbag to hit, the kids told me Abuser was usually calmer, giving them some respite too. When having seen me suffer enough to leave, Abuser wanted their punchbag back. In Abuser's case, sometimes with messages they had taken 'Valerian' (calming tablets) and it was safe to come home. This day they chose something different because if I left now I would have

another flat to stay in. The difference they chose, was a threat to kill the kids. It was too serious a threat for me to ignore. Refusing to abandon them to such a fate, I cancelled the viewing."

Victim's SMS, 22nd October 2012, 17.04

Hi. Sorry for any inconvenience but have been asked to stay longer at current address. Best regards, Victim.

"Their reply was kind and understanding and that was that, as far as my escape was concerned. It seemed I was going nowhere."

Chapter 20

Trapped Anew

"Now unable to even move out for fear of the kids' safety, Abuser used the opportunity to escalate their aggressions towards me. It was no longer every few days but several times a day, with the 'excuse' of 'my affair' and for making them so miserable. They knew I sometimes recorded them and, on this day, 24th October 2012, they were recording me too - while trying to get me to 'confess' to things I hadn't done. When I refused their ever louder demands, they slapped me so hard my entire body went sidewards – then they stormed out of the room. A moment later, obviously without any fear of reprisal, they strolled back in, announcing they had been recording. I told them I had too and mine was video. They said 'Good' but they weren't happy."

It is hard to understand what Abuser is trying to achieve with any of this, beyond their need to put Victim down and feed on their misery, regardless of family cost. There is no attempt at any positive or constructive outcome. It is interesting they resorted to a tactic of entrapment, trying to elicit a false confession on record, in effect trying to set Victim up.

I also see it as significant that, even after hitting Victim, they show no fear of retaliation. Even when they are recording, in an attempt to capture Victim bad behaviour, they are still unable to contain their rage. I wonder if they would have if they knew Victim was recording too. In either case, they clearly feel safe to abuse him, which is significant because of what Abuser will claimed just days later.

"The next day, Thursday 25th, I had booked another couple's counselling session. Craig, our pained counsellor, found all progress had become undone. Abuser began offloading about my lie of going to Kraków and their assertion I'd had an affair. I explained it had been to visit an ill friend, that the tickets had been booked while having to sleep in my car after being told to fuck off, crash and die, get a divorce and go away for longer – or at least that is what I tried to say. Abuser wound themselves up so much they stood up and, as they stormed past me for for the door, they deliberately hit me in the head – which Craig saw. His response was instant: 'Sorry, I can't deal with you any more Not with behaviour like that.' Even our counsellor feared to be in the same

room as the monster I and the kids had to live with, secretly abused behind closed doors."

This act of physical violence, even with such a witness present, can be explained in two ways. One, the abuser is so enraged they simply can't contain themselves. Two, they think they can get away with it, having got away with it so many times before. The counsellor saw it but the only consequence for Abuser was for them to be kicked out. For Abuser this was actually a positive outcome, the removal of someone questioning their behaviour.

"On Friday, 26th, while the kids were at school, Abuser was attacking me again - still demanding Agata's number and still trying to get me to admit to an affair that had never happened, though by now I wished it had. At least then I would have had sex and deserved the accusations. To Abuser's annoyance, I still refused to give in, so they got even angrier, ranting and raging until they had to go to work.

They stormed out of the house - it was over for now. I heard the sound of their car revving and driving off, then a crash. As I ran to a window I heard another crash, this time with breaking glass. Looking out I saw their car, nose to nose with mine in the drive, now reversing away. Activating the camera on my phone I tried to video them but it was in photo mode with no time to change setting. All I could do was watch them drive away, as the lady next door ran out to see what had happened. After the sound of breaking glass, I imagined smashed headlights on my car and called the police."

Police control centre log, 26/10/212 13:39

Method received: 999 call - - - Telephone No.: 02XXXX

Incident Detail: MY XXXX HAS RAMMED MY CAR TWICE BEFORE THEY LEFT FOR WORK... THIS HAS HAPPENED JUST NOW... THEY ARE XXXX.

Updates

13.40 YMC16, CALLER STATES XXXX HAS PREVIOUSLY DAMAGED THE CAR...

13.45 CVR4, M32 DESPATCHED

13.57 CVR3, M32 ARRIVED AT INCIDENT

15.27 OASIS, THE COUPLE ARE CURRENTLY HAVING MARRIAGE

PROBLEMS AND TODAY A VERBAL ARGUEMENT TOOK PLACE. THE I.P. - WHO IS THE FEMALE PARTY (an error of habit? It is the male who is the injured party) HAS LEFT THE ADDRESS IN A HURRY. DURING THIS THE I.P. HAS ORIGINALLY STATED THAT SHE HAS 'RAMMED' HIS VEHICLE. THERE WAS NO DAMAGE TO THE CAR (also incorrect) AND IT WOULD APPEAR THAT AS SHE HAS LEFT IN A RUSH SHE HAS EITHER STALLED HER CAR OR MADE CONTACT WITH HIS VEHICLE WHICH WAS ON THE DRIVE WAY.

HIS CALL TO US WAS FOR HELP REFERENCE HIS WIFE ISSUES AND HIS CONCERNS FOR HER POTENTIAL MENTAL HEALTH PROBLEMS. THE I.P. WAS ADVISED AND SIGN POSTED ACCORDINGLY. MALE I.P. IS VICTIM XXXX BN XXXX. OFFENDER FEMALE IS ABUSER XXXX BN XXXX. TWO CHILDREN XXXX

15.29 CVR3, All Resources Leave Scene-Dispatch Cancelled...

15.31 CVR3, Extra Details pasted on Incident Log...

Final Classification: PUBLIC SAFETY/WELFARE DOMESTIC INCIDENTS

Qualifier: DOMESTIC ABUSE

PC Lucy's report of this same incident ended with:

HE WAS ADVISED TO SEE HIS GP.

Crime interests: CHILD ABUSE OTHER

"When PC Lucy arrived and saw no visible damage on the front of the car, unbeknown to me, she incorrectly logged that it was probably just accidentally clipped on Abuser's way to work. I had mentioned but not emphasised the visible damage at rear, where my car had been pushed back through the six-foot wooden gate, splitting the wood, as well as scraping along the brickwork of the house. I was too relived the sound of breaking glass hadn't been my headlights but Abuser's and too focused on Abuser's out-of-control behaviour to focus on my car. After explaining our marital issues, PC Lucy kindly came and waited outside our school, literally just down the road, while I went inside and took the kids out early. It was the Friday before half term so my plan was to take the police officer's advice and go to our GP for help and then send the children to my mum, while me and Abuser sorted things between us - without them having to suffer it all."

Have kids and taking them to granny while we sort ourselves out. Called police after you rammed my car as you need mental help. They aren't going to arrest you for it. Can meet you tomorrow in neutral place to talk. Maybe go to talk to Natasha and stay there tonight. I'm not home today. Kids are fine. Didn't tell them anything except we need to sort ourselves out. xx

"I didn't tell Abuser the kids were being collected by train, with my mum making a 150 mile trip to collect them. If I did Abuser would have come to the train station and kicked off in front of the kids - exactly the kind of confrontation I was sending them away to avoid. Instead I gave misinformation, to make them think I was driving them there. In reality after my mum took them to safety, thanks to the GP's urgent referral, I was called by the Crisis Team - to discuss how to get help. Something had to change. We couldn't go on as we were. I assumed they would come to mediate, providing a safe, controlled environment to talk in."

Victim's SMS to Abuser, 26/10/2012, Fri, 15.21

Will call on landline shortly.

15.39

Home by 6.

Email from Abuser to Victim's mother, 26th October 2012, 3.43pm

Please bring my kids back to me as what you are doing is a kidnap. I don't wish them to be at your place with a very dirty and unsafe dogs around.

Forced to call police. You cheated on me, spent 4 days in Krakow and now playing some dirty games to hurt me using kids. I am the only one who sacrifices my life to have them... They are mine and always will be.

'...They are mine and always will be.' this is Abuser talking about the children as if they are possessions not people.

Victim's SMS to Abuser, 26/10/2012, Fri, 15.47

Driving.

16.19

Home this eve. We need to talk

> Driving.

I have just reported you to police, don't be surprise if somebody will come to visit you tomorrow.

Applying for divorce, and submitting Location Order application through CAFCASS which will apply directly to you.

"My mum wasn't picking up any of Abuser's emails at this time, she was on the train, doing her best to safeguard the kids."

> Granny taking kids to nice place

> Delayed. Home about 21.30.

"I had been granted an emergency meeting with a senior GP, Dr Gillian, who I knew from the patient panel meetings I was a member of. Abuser was also known as they worked as an interpreter for their Russian and Polish-speaking patients. I had also been to Dr Gillian and Dr Jane previously, regarding concerns about Abuser's rages and for advice on how to deal with them. Whether any of this helped I don't know but, either way, Dr Gillian had taken the events I described very seriously and sent the emergency referral to the local Crisis Team."

Thinks bi-polar disorder

Behaviour – strange, violent + angry, at times stubbing out cigarette on his head.

Thinks they're a Formula 1 driver, often drives into other things.

Thinks can hire out Warwick Castle. Spends lots on www.

Earlier in week said will kill children + herself...

This is quite a significant list of points. It covers violence, aggression and threats to kill, as well as delusions of grandeur and other behavioural concerns. The threats to kill alone are enough to warrant intervention.

"After my mum had travelled over 150 miles, at her own expense, to collect the kids and take them back to her place for safety, the phones call I got from the Crisis Team weren't offering mediation but asking me whether I would agree to Abuser being assessed under the Mental Health Act. It wasn't the path I wanted but it was the only help on offer and maybe it was what they needed. I was at a loss for what else to do so agreed – something had to change. What would you have done in my place?"

From the Mental Health Act 2007

Mental disorder is defined as *'any disorder or disability of mind'*. This definition includes conditions such as schizophrenia, depression, bipolar disorder, anxiety disorder, obsessive-compulsive disorder, eating disorders, personality disorders, autistic-spectrum disorders, organic disorders such as dementia, behavioural changes due to brain injury and mental disorders due to drug use. The definition includes learning disability only where it is associated with *abnormally aggressive or seriously irresponsible behaviour.*

There is a huge problem with such short assessments: lying. Those with a narcissistic personality disorder are world leaders at having their lies believed, especially when they know the system and what to say.

"I had been instructed not to go home but to wait for Abuser to be assessed. Wanting to be present at the assessment, still wanting mediation and discussion rather than any mental health lock up, I arranged to meet the Crisis Team near our house at 9.30pm, before they went to it. In the meantime, Abuser had got home to find the TV gone (I put it in my car to avoid them smashing it) as well as the children and several other possessions. Punchbag gone too, they began calling me and then the police, harassing them with claims I, a parent with equal rights, had kidnapped them and sent them to a stranger with dangerous dogs. The same 'stranger' Abuser had no qualms about them staying with four times already that year, with friendy dogs they loved to play with."

Extract of police control centre log, 26/10/212 16.23

Method received: 999 call - - - Telephone No.: 02XXXX

Incident Detail: MY EX PARTNER (actually husband and still living together) HAS PICKED UP MY CHILDREN FROM SCHOOL... THEY ARE AT HIS MOMS... THIS HAS NOT GONE THROUGH COURTS

ABOUT CUSTODY

Incident Result: ADVICE GIVEN.

Updates

16.50 CVC5, HAVE TRIED TO EXPLAIN TO THIS FEMAL ABOUT EQUAL PARENTAL RIGHTS- SHE IS NOT HAPPY WITH THIS STATED THAT HER HUSBAND COULD HAVE TAKEN HER KIDS TO HER MOTHER IN LAW AS SHE HAS 4 DOGS.

NOT HAPPY WITH THIS. STATED UK LAW IS CRAP SHE WILL TAKE HER CHILDREN AWAY.

Final Classification: PUBLIC SAFETY/WELFARE CONCERN FOR SAFETY

Qualifier: NONE.

Crisis Team Log, 26/10/2012, 17.50

Tel call to Abuser's husband. He reports that Abuser has been presenting as 'manic' on and off for years, she has no formal mental health diagnosis however and has never been on any medication for her mental health apart from Valium that she obtains via the Internet (actually it was Valerian, obtained over the counter in Latvia). Mr Ford states that he does not feel safe at the moment as Abuser is aggressive towards him and for that reason is not actually at home. He confirmed that the children were currently staying with their grandparents.... Due to the information on the initial referral I asked if Mr Ford felt a formal Mental Health Act assessment was required or if a CR/HT could conduct a generic visit at present... it was agreed that CR/HT would attempt to visit in the first instance...

Plan 1) H/V at 21.30... to assess the situation. Please phone Mr Ford first who will meet outside the property.

"At 9.30pm the Crisis Team members arrived and I sat in their car, playing a recording from 15th August 2012, where Abuser could be heard ranting in front of distressed kids.

Abuser, working as an interpreter for social services, knew exactly how the Crisis Team process worked and refused to open the door when we went there. Instead Abuser demanded my phone to be put through the letterbox, saying it was so they could call the kids, as granny was no longer answering their calls. Days later Abuser admitted they had wanted my phone so they could smash it. Crisis Team denied entry, I was instructed to stay away from the house until they could try again, the next day."

Crisis Team Log, 26/10/2012, 21.30

..we noticed that on the bay window inside the house there was a big banner which said that "MY HUSBAND IS A CHEAT". We knocked the door and Mrs Ford refused to open and Mrs Ford refused to open the door she spoke to us via the letter box and said she did not need CR/HT input and that she did not need our help she stated I don't smoke, I don't take drugs this is about what he has done he has cheated on me and has kidnapped my children and taken them to his mother house. Mrs Ford appeared and sounded extremely angry and accused her husband of cheating. We moved from the house with Mr Ford and sat in the car where Mr Ford played some recordings going back to August and September of Mrs Ford shouting and swearing and we could hear the children crying and screaming. Throughout the recording Mr Ford was never heard to say anything.

"It was unfortunate timing that Abuser had no credit left on their mobile. Instead they began calling me and everyone from the landline – stopped only on Sunday when we got cut off after they had run up a £150 bill, for me to pay.

Due to Abuser's lies about the kids being sent to a stranger with dangerous dogs, the local police did a welfare visit, where they found the kids safe and well, in a good environment with friendly dogs. The kids loved those dogs and had stayed at granny's place many times, even while Abuser and I flew to Latvia for their niece's wedding in July that year. Did the police welfare visit stop Abuser's wild claims about the children's safety? No – Abuser still wasn't back in control so kept calling."

Victim's SMS, 26/10/2012, Fri, 22.19

Email me.

23.55

Will you give me the number for the guys you betrayed me with? Email it over unless you are a hypocrite

"Had forgotten I wrote this until re-reading these texts for this book. Abuser had been focused on cheating, not me, which is why they thought I had cheated too."

Abuser's Diary, 26th October 2012

Black day in my life.

In costa at 1.

"Abuser didn't have mobile credit to call me so was texting them with suggestions for neutral ground to talk."

11.33

Costa at 3.

14.02

Costa at 3.

14.08

I've asked Natasha to call Agata since you won't meet me.

"Natasha was Abuser's best friend and someone I had become close to as well, confiding in her about the difficulties in our marriage. I trusted her."

14.23

Emailed you kids voice message.

"Before the children left Coventry, I recorded them giving their thoughts on the situation at home. Because they expressed displeasure at Abuser's aggression, Abuser just replied I had made them say it."

15.04

In costa.

15.05

Will leave at 3.30 if you don't come.

15.19

Not putting phone through letterbox. If you want to talk to kids come to costa and use my phone there. Driving to Kent shortly. You have 20 mins.

"Abuser was phoning me from the landline – sadly no recordings but you can be sure it wasn't pleasant or reasonable."

> You have pushed too hard. Your unfair jealousy and keeping your mental ill health more important to you than us, the kids and the house. Will prove my innocence with Agata. Can you prove yours with those other guys?

16.24

> John (Abuser's brother) might visit you.

16.30

> Did you tell neighbours you said you would kill the kids or that you fucked another? Bet not.

Extract from Crisis Team Log, 27/10/2012, 11.00

> Abuser's brother (actually it was me) rang to say had received an email informing they had burnt his clothes and had contacted the police to inform them of kidnapping her children. Advised that we were planning to visit again at 5pm today.

"Abuser spent the weekend harassing the police, with relentless claims against me and my mum. Members of the Crisis Team were refused entry again on Saturday and I spent another night away from home, this time at their nephew Yarka's house in Leamington Spa. He was well aware of Abuser's rages, having sometimes suffered them himself."

Police control centre log, 27/10/2012 10.41

Method received: 999 call - - - Telephone No.: 02xxxxxxxxx

Incident Detail: MY CHILDREN HAVE BEEN KIDNAPPED I REPORTED IT YESTERDAY AND WASN'T TAKEN SERIOUSLY MY CHILDREN WERE TAKEN TO HIS MUMS BY HIM AND LEFT THERE

Incident Result: NO FURTHER POLICE ACTION REQUIRED.

Updates

10.45 LHC6, THERE IS 4 WILD DOGS THERE THEY WILL EAT MY CHILDREN I HOPE YOUR CHILDREN ARE KIDNAPPED I CURSE YOU THEY WILL I CURSE YOU THEY WILL...

CALLER CLEARED

11.01 CVF2, VICTIM IS AT CENTRAL NOW ASKING TO SEE

OFFICERS RE THIS MATTER AS HE HAS ISSUES WITH HIS EX WIFE – I WILL SEE IF OFFICER FREE AND UPDATE SHORTLY

11.27 CVF2, HAVE SPOKEN WITH VICTIM AT LENGTH WHO STATES THE CHILDREN ARE BOTH WELL AND STAYING WITH HIS PARENTS IN KENT... IT APPEARS OFFICERS ATTENDED THE ADDRESS YESTERDAY AND A DV NON CRIME NUMBER WAS ISSUED. VICTIM STATES HIS WIFE ABUSER IS HAVING SOME SORT OF MENTAL HEALTH EPISODE – WHICH HAS BEEN INCREASING RAPIDLY OVER LAST FEW WEEKS- CRISIS TEAM CONFIRM THEY ATTENDED THE ADDRESS THE ADDRESS AND SHE WOULD ONLY SPEAK TO THEM THROUGH THE LETTERBOX- THEY WILL BE RE-ATTENDING AT 1700 HRS TODAY TO ASSESS HER IN FULL. VICTIM STATES HE IS STAYING AT FORMULA ONE HOTEL TEMPORARILY AS HE HAD TO LEAVE YESTERDAY DUE TO THE SITUATION... AS CRISIS TEAM ARE ALREADY IN THE ASSESSMENT PROCESS- POLICE ARE NOT REQUIRED ANY FURTHER. ABUSER WILL NEED TO BE ADVISED THAT WE ARE AWARE HER HUSBAND HAS TAKEN THE CHILDREN TO HIS PARENTS AND THAT ANY ISSUES RAISED ARE A CIVIL MATTER

13.57 Incident detail: FOR THE THIRD TIME I WANT TO REPORT THE KIDNAP OF MY CHILDREN- MY HUSBAND HAS TAKEN THEM TO HIS MOTHERS

14.03 LHC5, CALLER WILL NOT LISTEN TO THE FACT THAT THIS IS A CIVIL MATTER AND SHE HAS ALREADY BEEN ADVISED OF THIS EARLIER. STATES SHE WILL BREAK INTO HER MOTHER IN LAWS AND STEAL THEM BACK-FIREDSTATES ENGLISH LAW IS RUBBISH

NFI CALLER OFF LINE

14.09 CVC3, CALLER AWARE THAT THIS IS A CIVIL MATTER HOWEVER FROM PREVIOUS LOG **SHE IS SUFFERING FROM MENTAL HEALTH PROBLEMS.**

ALSO SEE LOG 909 OF 27.10.12

16.33 YMC10, FURTHER CALL (from Abuser) STATING THAT THIS IS NOT A CIVIL MATTER...SHE WAS THEN RANTING ON THE PHONE TOLD ME SHE WAS GOING TO TAKE THE CHILDREN HOME AND FUCK THE UK SHE DOES NOT KNOW WHERE THE CHILDREN ARE AT THIS TIME SHE IS ASSUMING THAT THEY ARE AT HER HUSBANDS MOTHERS ADDRESS...

19.48 Incident detail: FURTHER CALL FROM THIS FEMALE SAYS

HER CHILDREN HAVE BEEN TAKEN FROM FROM HER BY HER PARTNER. SAYS HE IS UNDERTAKING A SMEAR CAMPAIGN AGAINST HER.

19.48 YMC5, SHE SAID SHE WORKED FOR SOCIAL SERVICES FOR 9 YEARS AND IS TOTALLY SANE PERSON. SAYS WANT POLICE TO SPEAK TO HER NOT CRISIS TEAM. BELIEVE ALREADY CALLED TODAY..

19.59 SHC6, CALL RECEIVED FROM VICTIM WOULD LIKE OFFICERS DEALING WITH THIS TO CONTACT HIM- STATES TAKEN CHILDREN TO HIS PARENTS AS WAS CONCERNED FOR THEIR SAFETY DUE TO WIFES MH STATE- AND STATES THAT SHE HAS THREATENED TO KILL THE CHILDREN AND HERSELF RECENTLY

20.02 CVC3, I HAVE ADVISED THIS FEMALE AT LENGTH...NO REASONING WITH HER AT ALL SHE HAS SAID SHE WILL RING US 50 MORE TIMES

20.25 CVC2, FURTHER CALL FROM CRISIS TEAM STATING THIS LADY'S HUSBAND HAS JUST CONTACTED THEM TO SAY HE IS GOING TO THE ADDRESS AND MEETING POLICE....

20.33 CVC2, CRISIS TEAM WERE UNDER THE IMPRESSION ABUSER HAD MAYBE GIVEN HER HUSBAND THE INFORMATION HOPING HE WOULD GO AND SEE HER. HAVE MADE CONTACT WITH VICTIM AND CONFIRMED POLICE ARE NOT ATTENDING THE ADDRESS AND ADVISED HIM POLICE ARE NOT ATTENDING AND ADVISED HIM NOT TO ATTEND AS HIS WIFE HAS BEEN PHONING POLICE THIS EVENING AND HER MOOD IS NOT GOOD. HE EXPLAINED HE COULD NOT GO TO THE ADDRESS WITHOUT ANYONE AS HE DIDN'T KNOW WHAT STATE OF MIND SHE WOULD BE IN. INTENDS TO GO TO THE ADDRESS TOMORROW AS NEEDS SOME BELONGINGS BUT HE WILL CONTACT POLICE AND CRISIS TEAM.

20.38 CVC2, TRYING TO CONTACT CRISIS TEAM BUT CONSTANTLY ENGAGED.

20.48 CVC2, CRISIS TEAM STILL BUSY

THEY ARE PROBABLY TALKING WITH ABUSER SO WILL CLOSE LOG...

Final Classifier: PUBLIC SAFETY/WELFARE CIVIL DISPUTE

Qualifier: NONE

Narcissists need to be in control. If faced with officials empowered to act against them, they will do anything and everything to avoid them, unless it is on their terms.

> Abuser. Stay calm and see you tomorrow. Xx

22.14

> Apart from you trashing my name even more am glad you are OK.

Crisis Team Log, 28/10/2012, 01.20

> T/C from Abuser in response to the letter left earlier. She stated she did not feel she has any mental illness but that she would see us as we had continued to contact her. Abuser stated that the problem was marital and that he had kidnapped the children and she didn't know where they were which had caused her terrible distress. She feels that her husband is trying to make her seem mentally ill and she feels humiliated by the whole situation.
>
> Abuser was rational throughout, but upset by the events of the last few days.
>
> I reassured her that we were aiming to offer her support and had not intended to add to her distress, she was grateful for our kindness and offers of support, even though she is not sure we can help or get her children back.
>
> PLAN: Assessment booked for 6pm...

Doesn't Abuser sound like a poor victim here? Just contrast the detail of what has been said with what they were telling the police. For example, they says they don't know where the children are yet they told the police they know they are with their grandmother. Also contrast what they told the police - that the children have no relationship with their grandmother and there are four dangerous dogs who will eat them - with Abuser asking the grandmother to look after the children for longer, after looking after them for a week in July while we flew to the wedding in Latvia, and then again in September. Not a single concern about dogs then or any notion of no relationship with their grandmother. And yet, for all Abuser's lies, they are believed and they manage to twist the situation to appear the victim.

Victim's SMS 28/10/2012, Sun, 09.53

> Will call again in an hour. Take care.

"I had no idea Abuser had called the Crisis Team themself, to begin their act of 'innocent victim'."

09.59

At work until 4. Can meet you in new costa at 4.20

"Still being responsible, I went to work. When you are on a zero-hours contract you can't afford not to."

17.27

will be in 10 mins.

17.48

Can't make it to costa either.

"I was giving more misinformation as wanted to get back to the house and grab some things while they was out. Couldn't. Abuser had already changed the lock."

Narcissists absolutely must feel in control. Victim had been denying Abuser that and now they were on the warpath to get it back. No matter what.

Police control centre log, 28/10/2012 18.13

Method received: Telephone call - - - Telephone No.: 07xxxxxxxxx

Incident Detail: REPORTING DOMESTIC AT LOCATION. CALLER HAS BEEN LOCKED OUT OF PREMISES BY WIFE WHO IS IN THERE. HE NEEDS TO GET POSSESSIONS WHICH SHE STATES SHE HAS TRASHED. NO CHILDREN AT LOCATION AS CALLER HAS TAKEN THEM TO KENT.

Updates

18.14 SHC4, CALLER IS SITTING IN HIS CAR ON THE DRIVEWAY.

18.15 SCH4, 5 PREVIOUS LOGS IN LAST 3 DAYS AT LOCATION

18.21 CVC7, CALLER HAS BEEN BACK ON...CRISIS TEAM PRESENT AND WIFE HAS ALLOWED THE ACCESS HE IS GOING TO TRY AND ENTER WHEN THEY COME OUT. I HAVE ADVISED HIM WE DON'T HAVE ANY UNITS AT PRESENT.

19.02 CVC2, CALL FROM CRISIS TEAM SOCIAL WORKER AT ADDRESS NOW. THEY ARE ATTEMPTING TO DO A MENTAL HEALTH ASSESSMENT ON THIS LADY AND HER HUSBAND IS

PEEKING THROUGH THE WINDOWS AND IMPEDING THEIR ASSESSMENT WITH THE LADY (Abuser) WHO IS VERY FRIGHTENED. THEY ARE ASKING IF THERE IS ANY ONE WHO CAN ATTEND..

19.29 SHC6, FURTHER CALL FROM VICTIM ASKING FOR OFFICERS TO ATTEND.

"On the Sunday I called the Crisis Team for an update and found their attitude had suddenly become very cold towards me, as if my even calling was harassing them. I was told Abuser had called them and arranged a meeting for that evening so said I would be there so we could all talk."

Chapter 21

Women Only

"Clearly focused on not listening to me"

"Being the end of October 2012, it was a cold evening as I sat in my car in the driveway, waiting for both the police, who I had asked to be present, and the Crisis Team members to attend. Abuser had changed the door lock and was inside with their best female friend and some female, eastern European Nazi I'd never seen before but who felt confident enough to come to the door and denounce me before locking me out again, of my own house. Not long after, two female members of the Crisis Team arrived and I went to talk to them.

Abuser was in full 'normal' mode and the Crisis Team, clearly focused on not listening to me, seemed more than happy to go along with them. They went inside, Abuser locking the door behind them. In what way was this any kind of mediation or balanced approach? How was anyone supposed to make a full assessment with the second party, the very person who had raised the concerns, being kept outside? In the video you can see me not just freezing outside but the damage to my office once allowed in."

Police control centre log, 28/10/2012 18.13

Method received: Telephone call - - - Telephone No.: 07XXXX

Incident Detail: REPORTING DOMESTIC AT LOCATION. CALLER HAS BEEN LOCKED OUT OF PREMISES BY WIFE WHO IS IN THERE. HE NEEDS TO GET POSSESSIONS WHICH SHE STATES SHE HAS TRASHED. NO CHILDREN AT LOCATION AS CALLER HAS TAKEN THEM TO KENT.

Updates

19.33 CVR4, M33 DESPATCHED

19.34 CVR4, M32 HAS KNOWLEDGE OF THIS COUPLE DUE TO PREVIOUS INCIDENT WILL PTP M33 WITH INFO

19.35 CVR3, M33 ARRIVED AT INCIDENT. UNIT WITH VICTIM NOW.

20.12 CVS3, UNIT ASKING FOR KENT POLICE TO DO A SAFE AND

WELL CHECK ON THE TWO CHILDREN FROM THIS ADDRESS...

20.36 CVC2, SORRY TO BE A PAIN BUT IS THERE A CONCERN FOR THE WELFARE OF THE CHILDREN? WHAT REASON SHALL I GIVE FOR THE REQUEST?

20.41 CVS3, THE CHILDREN HAVE BEEN TAKEN TO HIS MUMS BY THEIR FATHER AS THEIR MOTHER IS MENTALLY ILL. WE JUST NEED TO MAKE SURE THEY HAVE NOT COME TO ANY HARM WHILST AT THEIR HOME ADDRESS.

"**The police finally arrived - PC Stuart, the only male official to be present that night. PC Stuart went inside to find out what was going on. Minutes later, PC Lucy, the kind officer who had safeguarded the sending of the children to their grandmother on the Friday, arrived. She also went inside to see what was happening. Not long after, PC Stuart came out to talk to me.**

I felt the need for some support so played the officer the same August recording of Abuser kicking off. He seemed unimpressed. I told him Abuser hits me. He just shrugged: '*What do you want me to do about it?*' **Obviously he intended to do nothing.**

When I was finally allowed inside - only upstairs while Abuser, saying was stressed by my presence, stayed in the living room with the two social workers, female friend, female Nazi and two police officers, one female - I discovered my office had been trashed even more than before."

Not the first time Abuser had trashed Victim's home office.

101

"Abuser had thrown a lot of my other things in there too, including brand new leather boots, all with red paint tipped over it all – wedding photo included. I had my GoPro camera so began filming and asked the officers to come and take a look at this evidence of their aggression and abuse. PC Lucy, who downstairs had said it wasn't fair Abuser couldn't see their children, seemed quite taken aback but PC Stuart just said: *'Joint property'*, meaning he classified it as joint possessions so no criminal damage and no action necessary to help me with that either. Instead of questioning Abuser about it, I was repeatedly told to hurry up – apparently Abuser was giving an Oscar-winning performance of 'being stressed by my nasty presence' in my own house. Putting what few surviving office valuables I could into a bag, I left with my boots, still dripping red paint."

When an abuser is unable to enact their rage directly against their victim they enact it indirectly, against what ever is precious to them. This can be anything from possessions to loved ones, finances to career. Unlike normal people, they have no sense of moral compass, only the need to put down by inflicting pain. In Abuser's case here, even with their actions on full view for the police to see, no action was taken against them because, as documents will later reveal, they had already convinced everyone they were the victim.

This is the process I have referred to as DARVO: Deny, Attack and Reverse Victim and Offender; coined by Freyd at the University of Oregon. An evidently successful tactic used by Abuser, to make themselves appear the victim and the Victim, me, appear the abuser.

Freyd on DARVO

"...I have observed that actual abusers threaten, bully and make a nightmare for anyone who holds them accountable or asks them to change their abusive behaviour. This attack, intended to chill and terrify, typically includes threats of law suits, overt and covert attacks on the whistle-blower's credibility, and so on..... The offender rapidly creates the impression that they are the wronged one, and the victim or concerned observer is the offender... The offender is on the offence and the person attempting to hold the offender accountable is put on the defence." (Freyd, 1997).

Politicians do this too. Think of those who go heavily on the attack when accused of wrong doing, to deflect from having to answer the actual accusations, or repeat bare-faced lies to reporters.

"I went back outside, back to the cold October night – back to waiting outside for my turn to give my side of things. A moment

later PC Stuart came to join me but gave nothing in the way of support.

Even today, with all the claims of gender neutrality and the illegality of gender bias in all walks of life, there remain far too many cases of gender bias in both the police and social services – especially when it comes to domestic violence.

"After some time the two social workers came out and, instead of asking me for any information for my side of events or even saying anything regarding the next steps, they just walked past – ignoring me. Assessment over police wanted to leave, which meant they wanted me to leave to. Even though I was the one who had asked them to be there to assist me. It meant another night in a hotel, no further forward than two days ago."

DARVO: Deny, Attack, and Reverse Victim and Offender

The process where a perpetrator (Abuser) denies their attack and then attacks their victim (Victim) again by making others believe he was the attacker – effectively reversing victim and offender. This is exactly what Abuser has done here.

Police control centre log, 28/10/2012 18.13

Method received: Telephone call - - - Telephone No.: 07XXXX

Incident Detail: REPORTING DOMESTIC AT LOCATION. CALLER HAS BEEN LOCKED OUT OF PREMISES BY WIFE WHO IS IN THERE. HE NEEDS TO GET POSSESSIONS WHICH SHE STATES SHE HAS TRASHED. NO CHILDREN AT LOCATION AS CALLER HAS TAKEN THEM TO KENT.

Updates

21.51 OASIS, CST UPDATE RECORDED AS CHILD ABUSE NON-CRIME INCIDENT

21.51 CVS3, AWAITING UPDATE FROM KENT POLICE RE THE SAFE & WELL CHECK ON THE CHILDREN.

22.20 SFA1, I HAVE NOW RECEIVED A TELEPHONE CALL FROM KENT POLICE... THE CHILDREN ARE CURRENTLY IN BED ASLEEP. APPARENTLY THE SON COLLECTED THE CHILDREN AND HANDED THEM TO HIS MUM AND THERE APPEARS TO BE NO INJURY.

> **23.47 CVF1,** KENT POLICE HAVE RUNG STATING THEY HAVE VISITED ADDRESS AND SPOKEN TO GRANDMOTHER WHO STATED CHILDREN ARE SAFE AND WELL AND ARE ASLEEP AT PRESENT. OFFICERS WERE SATISFIED THEY ARE WELL LOOKED AFTER HOWEVER IF YOU WANT THEM TO RETURN TO THE ADDRESS IN THE MORNING TO SPEAK TO THE CHILDREN IN PERSON THEY ARE HAPPY TO DO SO.
>
> **00.08 CVS3** PS XXXX AWARE & HAPPY THAT WE DO NOT NEED TO ATTEND AGAIN TO SEE THE CHILDREN.
>
> **Final Classification:** PUBLIC SAFETY/WELFARE CONCERN FOR SAFETY
>
> MENTAL HEALTH/VULNERBALE CHILDREN/YOUNG PERSON

Crisis Team report: 28th October 2012

> Possible safeguarding issue with regard to her sons, aged 7 yrs and 8 yrs being taken to stay with grandmother who lives in Kent, by her husband without her knowledge. The children do not have a relationship with their grandmother and she is not allowing Abuser to even speak to them. Police have agreed to ask Kent police to carry out a safe and well check on the children. I will refer to social care first thing on the 29-10-12.

This was on the Sunday and purely for effect. Abuser knew a safe and well check had already been carried out by Kent police on the Friday and that it was totally unnecessary in the first place for there were no safety issues there. Abuser knew the children had a very good relationship with their grandmother and had been happy for them to stay there when it suited their needs.

The whole picture they had painted for the Crisis Team was a totally false one, which sadly the Crisis Team seems only too happy to support. Note the Crisis Team's phrasing of: *'by her husband **without her knowledge'**.* Both parents have equal parental responsibility so neither party needs permission of the other to make such a decision and, given the context of the children being sent to their grandmother, would it not have made more sense to focus on the issues that had led to the referral in the first place? Such as Abuser's threats to kill the children?

"It took until a court hearing the following August before I got a copy of the paperwork from that day and saw the extent of what Abuser had said against me that day and how badly the Crisis Team had handled things. Furious, I put in a formal complaint.

Back in 2012, after the Crisis Team left, Abuser started to call me again – only now I was not in a mood to talk."

104

Will bring kids to cov in few days and tell you when.

22.05

Am cancelling rent transfer and all bill payments since no longer live there. Will tell agency have left but won't tell you have damaged the property etc. Am not nasty like you.

22.07

Going to find a kind a sane woman.

"Agata had reminded me there was a world with pleasant, caring people out there and that was where I wanted to go. How naive I was to think was in any position to do anything I wanted for myself."

22.08

You could have talked to me when was there freezing for 2 hours. Fudge off.

22.11

Phone bill yours now too.

22.11

Stop calling.

23.15

At some point need to collect the rest of my stuff. We can organise it with police one morning when back in Cov. Cancelled all utility payments and giving you as sole payee. They will write to you.

Victim's SMS 29/10/2012 Mon 09.21

Please bring 2 sets of clothes for kids. Can meet 11 or 12 in centre.

Chapter 22

Abuser Calls

"You're fucked", Abuser

"Monday morning I got a phone call from Abuser: 'You need to give me the kids back'. I said not before we resolve what is going on between us. Abuser told me: 'You don't understand. They think you are an abuser and will give me custody if you don't do what I say.' I was stunned. Even by their standards this was a nightmare. We arranged to meet."

Still think females are powerless against males? This situation is far from unique. For while male abusers will mostly get caught for using physical violence, female and the more devious male abusers will tend to use psychology and lies to get what they want. By the time their chosen victims - usually chosen for being tolerant, honest, loving people – start to understand the callousness and cold-blooded depth of actions being taken against them, they are already a hundred steps behind. As fast as they try to get their heads around the actions being taken against them, by their supposed loved ones, they can never catch up. No amount of protesting on their side will help for, in terms of the actions now afoot, they are not players but passengers, carried by the abusers tidal wave of hate, sweeping away all fairness and truth from what is now a living hell.

Transcript, 29/10/2012, 12.50, café -

Abuser	You're fucked. *(not yet uploaded or transcribed further)*

"What Abuser told me was as shocking as it was awful. 'I had to put you down to put myself up', they told me, openly admitting they had lied to the Crisis Team and made them believe I was the abuser. Rather than retract it, they still used their increased power to force me to do as they said or they would use it against me.

Most of the rest of that day is a blur. I remember we went to child social services, for Abuser to assure them everything was now OK so they no longer needed to be involved. Abuser found such involvement embarrassing and, on reflection, it also carried the risk of their true nature coming out.

At social services around 4pm, I was still in shock and furious. My assertions of innocence seemed to come as a total shock to them – for no-one else had asked my side of events. It didn't

106

matter though, at the end of the day, my parental control was under serious threat and I had to surrender or lose the children.

I had lost the battle and Abuser took full advantage of it to make me drive us 180 miles to granny's in Kent, to drag the kids, aged only 6 and 7 out of bed at 11pm. Granny had offered to let us stay and take them calmly in the morning after they had slept and had breakfast but Abuser was on a mission to punish granny too. As for the welfare of the children, this parent social services had chosen to fully empower, couldn't have cared less. Abusre considered them their possessions and their's alone, to do with exactly as they wished."

Keeping Children in Harm's Way

By automatically believing the tearful woman, in keeping with Women's Aid's stance on domestic violence gender bias, and not even bothering to ask the husband a single question, the Crisis Team empowered the abusive mother to further harm their children. Despite this mother's threat to kill the children being on record in the GP's emergency referral.

"Driving home, with Abuser verbally hammering me in the car and two under slept, upset kids having to hear it all in the back, I pulled over at the first motorway services for coffee and a break. I didn't want to go home. I didn't want to go anywhere with Abuser. I wanted out but had tried to get help to protect the kids and all I had got was the threat of losing custody.

When we had finally covered the 180 miles home again, the kids went inside and Abuser refused me entry to our house. They had used me to get what they wanted, their hook: our kids. Before I was allowed back in they demanded the return of their passports – which had taken to prevent Abuser's threat of vanishing them abroad, to Dubai or Russia – neither had an extradition treaty with the UK.

If we were on a desert island I would have shoved Abuser out the way and told them to go screw themself but we weren't. We were in England, supposedly the land of justice for all but with zero justice for me or the children. It was one of the lowest points of my life. Thinking back, I really don't know how I managed to go on, except I had to. My kids needed me. They didn't deserve to be left alone, in the clutches of the Devil incarnate. The battle had been lost, but the war wasn't over.

The next day I awoke glum yet determined. Abuser was still enjoying their new level of power over me and I resolved to fight back, by recording us 24/7. Having worked as an undercover journalist for Channel 4's Dispatches, I had the skills to do this and the knowledge of needing the full picture.

If I only tried to record Abuser kicking off, they could lie I had provoked them, but if I was recording all the time, I could evidence there had been no provocation.

Have you any idea how hard it is to record 24/7? To log events, avoid flat batteries, data loss or device discovery? Many times I recorded them openly, mostly when they were kicking off.

'I'm recording'

At first this helped calm them down. They knew the recordings could prove they were the abuser so controlled themself. Then, when they realised I hadn't been taking the recordings to the authorities, they simply got used to them and carried on regardless. It didn't stop them grabbing for the recorder or trying to smash it but, with their aggression being recorded while they were trying to do so. I was able to use my strength to physically keep them back, without them being able to lie I was abusing them by doing so."

Chapter 23

Revenge on Dr Gillian

"I want you to leave now. Please leave", Dr Gillian

"Our children were returned home to more abuse by Abuser. And they were dragged into the campaign of revenge against others that had dared to challenge their behaviour. In this case it was Dr Gillian, the kind-hearted GP who had taken Abuser's abnormal behaviour seriously when I asked for help.

We arrived at the surgery, children in tow, and Abuser asked to speak to Dr Gillian about what had happened. The receptionist went to Dr Gillian's surgery room and returned to say Abuser's request had been declined and they should make an appointment. Did Abuser accept that reply? No. If it wasn't an answer Abuser wanted it wasn't an answer Abuser would accept so they strode Dr Gillian's surgery room and went inside."

Despite being told no, Abuser pushed into Dr Gillian's room anyway. October 2012.

"As you can predict, Abuser was not pleasant to her. In fact Abuser became so aggressive, Dr Gillian not only asked them to leave but also hit the panic button under her desk – repeatedly."

Chapter 24

Abused Children

Our abuser was empowered to abuse them

"Empowered by the Crisis Team and their abysmal failure to deal with the true culprit, it wasn't just me left at the hands of the abuser it was our children too. It wasn't just they abused me in front of them, they would try and elicit their support in the abuse. What is the point of Woman's Aid banging on about the negative effects of abusers on children, while effectively supporting abusers to keep hold of their children and keep abusing them?"

Paul and Alan, at a happy time. Both adults now, they refuse to talk to Abuser.

Crisis Team letter to Dr Gillian, 31ˢᵗ October 2012

...XXXX was referred to our team via SPE on 26/10/2012. She was referred by her husband who raised concerns that she was suffering from bi-polar disorder.

There have been relationship issues with their marriage, which appears to be causing them both high levels of distress to the point that husband took two children away without her knowledge.

I assessed Abuser on 28/10/2012 and could find no evidence to suggest that she was suffering from any mental health problems apart from the stress of having her two young children taken away to stay with their grandmother in Kent without her knowledge or consent...

This is what happens when only one side of an argument is listened to and the abuser gets free reign to lie their socks off, without question or evidence. Whether it can be put down to poor training, gender bias or both the end result is the same: the abuser is empowered to abuse the children and partner even more. Which is exactly what Abuser did.

Chapter 25

Divorce, No Divorce

"I'll make you arrested and escorted from this house", Abuser

5 months before escape

"One evening, as Abuser was demanding divorce, I agreed to it so they moved the goal posts, by adding threats of arrest based on lies."

Abuser's threats of divorce were simply a power-play put down. When abuse is not deemed to be causing suffering or hurt, they change their tactics. This can seen in the transcript of this event, below.

Transcript, 12th November 2012, 8.10pm, kitchen/diner -

ABUSER	You know if you don't like something fudge off
VICTIM	No, I said it (let's divorce) in a very nice way.
ABUSER	Very nice way. So let's finish then in a very nice way. Fuck off then. But actually not in a nice way. I'll make you arrested and escorted from this house.
VICTIM	For what?
ABUSER	Well. Plenty of reasons. Such a piece of shit like you without brain. I'm sure I will think of somehow. And one more glass of anything in this house and alcoholics anonymous crisis team are coming here too. Well there isn't actually a crisis team at alcoholics anonymous but there is a help which can be reported by any member of the family too. And I knew every body (who came) for (the) assessment.
VICTIM	They can come and assess me.
ABUSER	Yeah they can yeah it's not a problem.
VICTIM	What, I had two beers yesterday?
ABUSER	I also will call your employer, don't worry.
VICTIM	Won't they laugh at you? Two. What he had two beers after his night shift? Wow, big deal.
ABUSER	No that you're beating me. Or further.

First, Abuser states they knew everyone who came to assess them so, in

113

what possible way, was it a fair assessment or one professionally conducted?

Second, the willingness with which Abuser states they are willing to make false claims to the police against Victim. This is typical of abusers and, without recorded evidence, can simply come down to who the police believe the most. As many male victims will tell you, something the statistics seem to bear out, more often than not the male is the one not believed. Working as an interpreter for social services, Abuser very much knew this.

The 12th November 2012 transcript continues:

ALAN	Mummy. Mummy. Mummy. Mummy you said you would kill everyone. That means you'll kill Paul and me.
ABUSER	No
VICTIM	Actually actually Alan you should know mummy actually said that. That's why I didn't move house two weeks ago.
ABUSER	One time and daddy was dropping you on the stairs
VICTIM	And mummy and mummy's just agreed. Did you hear that? She didn't deny it.
ABUSER	One time I said that I understand a woman who done it to her children
VICTIM	No you said directly that you would kill Alan and Paul yourself.
ABUSER	No I did not.
VICTIM	Yes you did, I've got it recorded.
ABUSER	No I did not
VICTIM	I've got it recorded. Do you want to hear the recording?
ABUSER	Nobody gives a shit about your recordings.
VICTIM	Do you want me to play it to the kids?
ABUSER	And nobody will be ever listening to your recordings do you understand. You can even put them on the TV, nobody will be listening to them. And actually everybody is laughing about your recordings. Even social worker knows. Even she's written that you're paranoid by recording everyone and everything and it's been highlighted many times by me you're working for TV, now you're unsuccessful in your job so you're recording me instead.

114

	Because you can't stop sneaking like a parasite behind people's back. You know what you were doing for Channel 4 (Dispatches) is also very humiliating because actually work for bloody very, very dodgy people without any honesty and niceness.

"Interestingly, when I was working for Channel 4, Abuser was really pleased – both because of the television status and the money. The daily rants against me were simply to put me down. Logically I knew they were wrong, with all the negative things they kept saying, but deep down I could feel it sinking into my psychology – like water soaking through chalk and pooling underneath."

The 12th November 2012 transcript continues:

ABUSER	You know what the fact that you were just concentrating on one sentence I told in my life entire life shows how perfect I am.
VICTIM	What?
ABUSER	Well you just grabbed into one sentence oh 'I said I'd kill myself and kids' and it's quite funny you completely don't see the whole picture how much damage you've done by your drinking and by your behaviour and by not supporting your family and you grabbed one sentence and fucking around in Poland and just generally
VICTIM	What fucking around in Poland?
ABUSER	OK not (Abuser had accepted I hadn't had an affair)
VICTIM	You're calling me an alcoholic. Bloody hell. I'm going out driving a car now and you're going to call me an alcoholic now?
ABUSER	Where are you going now?
VICTIM	To get some space.
ABUSER	From kids, yeah? Kiddies daddy doesn't like you. Doesn't want to be with you.
PAUL	What?
ABUSER	Daddy is going away as usual. Running away from the family.
ALAN	Forever?
VICTIM	No no no. Daddy's just going out for a little bit
ABUSER	Oh yes, for a while, because he can't stand us.

VICTIM	Mummy's just talking rubbish. I can't stand being hammered.
ABUSER	No, you can't stand us. Because he can't stand the truth, frankly speaking.
VICTIM	Or your version of the truth.
ABUSER	My version? I've been beaten. I've been bloody abused by alcoholic. Why would I make it up?
VICTIM	Don't know. Why would you make it up?
ABUSER	Because I didn't. Because it's truth and you just can't swallow this.
VICTIM	Yeah but to you two beers in a weekend is an alcoholic.
ABUSER	You can't swallow this. Can you? You can't admit that you fucked up so badly so badly that I'm still in shock
VICTIM	Yeah sometimes I do. Sometimes I screwed up and I said sorry for it but you weren't perfect either.
ABUSER	Well once times sorry is enough, oh yeah supposed to make up for everything. He said sorry...
VICTIM	I'm not entirely to blame.
ABUSER	Yes, of course you're not. Yes you are. Yes you are.
VICTIM	No I'm not.
ABUSER	Yes, you are. Yes, you are. Yes, you are.

"When I look back at these transcripts, I can hear their voice in my head as if am still there. Still being ruined by this maniac. How the hell did I survive all this without going mental or just gagging them for peace? Nothing I said or did made any difference. When they didn't have something to use against me they invented something or warped an account to suit their own ends."

Abuser's Diary, 18th November 2012

Latvia – fucking country.

"Abuser was always very critical of the high rate of nationalism in Latvia, their country of birth, and had even inspired me to make a documentary on it – with Abuser as the presenter. Later, when it suited them, they bemoaned my criticisms of their country, as if they hadn't been the one inspiring them nor the key player."

Chapter 26

Our Children Speak

"If they love me why do they shout at me?", Alan

"With almost open warfare from Abuser and separation looking imminent, while they were out, I sat the children down after school to ask what they wanted. Social services might have called this an inappropriate question for a 7 and 8-year-old, but to me it was important the children had a voice in their futures. They hadn't been given a choice in who their mother chose to be so they deserved a voice on what happened next, including Abuser's idea of taking them to Latvia, which made Alan ask *'What about our friends?'*. Paul began commenting on mummy's rages while Alan looked concerned, this is where the transcript begins."

Transcript 20th November 2012, 17.07, kitchen-diner -

VICTIM	Paul, I said don't think about what mummy and daddy might want. What do you want?
ALAN	(very quietly/sadly) No shouting.
VICTIM	No shouting...
ALAN	(wipes his eyes on his shirt)
VICTIM	Paul, what do you really want?
PAUL	I don't know... I can't decide between you two.
VICTIM	What do you want most in your life, Paul?
PAUL	What do you mean?
VICTIM	Do you feel safe with mummy and daddy? Do you feel safe with daddy? Safe with mummy?
PAUL	I feel safe with you.
VICTIM	What makes you feel not safe with mummy?
PAUL	(mimics someone shouting, with a very open mouth)
	Watch the recording to see more.

"Several months before this, when returning to Coventry from their summer holiday with granny and Tony, my step-father, at the

thought of going back home to Abuser's rages, Alan told granny: *'I wish our mum would die, so we can live in peace.'* He was just seven years old. Granny was shocked by this, mostly because it was so sad for a young child to feel so traumatised by his abusive parent's behaviour that he wanted them dead, just to make the torment stop."

Much the same as Victim enjoyed the normality of the time with Agata, Alan had enjoyed the normality of their time with granny and Tony. No shouting. No arguments. A chance to live, as a child in a happy environment but knowing the environment he was returning to and dreading it. In 2012, it wasn't illegal to be coercively aggressive nor inflict raging rants, but it was immoral and totally unacceptable behaviour, especially in front of children. Alan's desperate need for Abuser's shouting to stop shows just how damaging it was being to him.

As mentioned earlier, in June 2020, Professor Nicola Graham-Kevan gave a speech, stating that in actual fact, there are **more male abuse victims than female abuse victims.**
Six years before this, in June 2014, Theo Merz wrote a piece in the Telegraph, entitled: *"Women are more 'controlling and aggressive than men' in relationships"*

It is such a shame the Crisis Team didn't do a proper assessment the month before. If they had, such suffering could have already been resolved. Instead they empowered the abuser, disempowered the victim and made the whole situation even worse.

By empowering abusers to keep abusing, officials further abuse the children, potentially turning them into future abusers or victims.

Chapter 27

I Will Kill All of Us

"Try to hit me back, I'll call the police", Abuser

"Faced with my increasing library of recorded evidence against them, Abuser lay next to me in bed and, thinking I wasn't still recording, repeated their threat against the children's lives."

Transcript 22nd November 2012, 4.07am, in bed -

VICTIM	You very specifically said...
ABUSER	And I say this again. Yes I do understand.
VICTIM	Yes but from that
ABUSER	It's better to kill myself and children than let children to live without me. So if you will ever attempt to separate me with children, yes, I will kill all of us.

"What kind of parent even thinks such things about any child, let alone their own?"

A narcissist is very good at working out what their victim cares about and then using it to control them. In this case, Abuser is clearly threatening Victim against going back to the authorities, by threatening to harm the people they care most about: their children.

Transcript 22nd November 2012, 5.16am, in bed -

ABUSER	And I will set you up. Oh I'll fucking set you up. You can't leave me alone in nice way and fuck off from my life. Fine I will do it in grandiose way. With police arrest
VICTIM	For what?
ABUSER	You in jail.
VICTIM	For what? Stop hitting me. Fucking hell!
ABUSER	For this.
VICTIM	You just kicked me onto the floor.
ABUSER	Try to hit me back, I'll call police.
VICTIM	Fucking maniac. And you wonder why I chose to get the Crisis Team involved.

Here we see how empowered and untouchable Abuser feels. Despite being the abuser and threatening to kill the children, it has been clearly demonstrated that the authorities will believe they are the victim. They have been empowered to abuse at will and Victim is all too aware that if they dare go back to the authorities they have to be 100% sure they don't lose. We can also see how well Abuser has chosen their victim, for Victim doesn't lose their temper and retaliate but puts up with it, seething in silence.

"I was furious and frustrated but knew exactly how they would present it if the police were called and how likely they would be to take action against me rather than them – even with the recording. With their threats to kill the children, there could be no half measures. I had to be sure I had enough to prove they were the abuser and real danger to them, not the sobbing victim they could play so well. I had to bide my time. The saving grace was the fact I had been recording that and had just got more evidence of their abuse."

I have a theory that narcissists are such good liars because they can almost believe their own lies. Having zero empathy for their victims, they have zero moral restraint on how deeply they will lie.

Abuser's Diary, end of November 2012

The reason people find is so hard to be happy is that they always see the past better than it was. The present worse than it is and the future less resolved than it will be.

"Does Abuser mean: resolved by me being dead?"

Chapter 28

Solicitor

"Either you promise to take action on this or I will", solicitor

"Needing help but knowing it was too risky to simply go back to the authorities, I made an appointment at Citizen's Advice and they booked me in with their visiting solicitor, Caroline. In that meeting, I played the solicitor the very same recording of Abuser kicking off in front of the children I had played the Crisis Team and PC Stuart. Unlike them, her response was immediate and strong within 15 seconds flat: *'There is obviously something not right with her. I have a duty of care so either you promise to take action on this and tell me when you have or I will.'*

I was relieved someone agreed there was something very wrong with Abuser, though also at a loss as to what to do next, after promising the solicitor I would take action. What action could I take without things being turned against me again? Thankfully, Caroline told me: 'As a victim of domestic violence, you can get Legal Aid for a solicitor and the police have a dedicated domestic violence unit. Go and talk to them.'"

This shows the vast difference and pot-luck as to how seriously domestic violence against can be taken. If the Crisis Team or PC Stuart had acted with the same attitude towards it, the children and Victim could have been saved months of Abuser's escalated aggression.

"I left the meeting, brain burning with gladness of being believed and concern for how to go forward without things again being turned against me. It wasn't long after that I began looking into solicitors who accepted Legal Aid and chose one. Even back then, in 2012, there weren't many that still did so.

Things at home had been getting worse, with open discussions of divorce as well as daily attempts to kill me via sleep deprivation.

'I want you to crash and die.', **were the cold-blooded words the children and I would hear every night before I left for work - so under slept I would try to leave early, to have a catnap in the car or van before it started.**

I found a solicitors not far from the main police station and made an appointment. On the day of that appointment, after my

chat with the solicitor, Steve, who agreed to take on my case, I was standing in their reception sorting a full booking when in walked Abuser. They had come to see a solicitor too and was surprised to see me there. They were also visibly annoyed when the receptionist realised we were spouses and had to turn them away to avoid conflict of interest. I was glad. Finally I was getting some back up, though wondered how they would be at home. Although things at home were now so bad, how could they possibly get any worse?"

The tactics abusers use include isolation from others. While Abuser had succeeded in mostly isolating Victim from friends and family, they knew they couldn't do the same with an appointed solicitor so had to think again.

"While Abuser was perhaps slightly less nasty than usual when I got home, perhaps to get more information from me as to what I was now planning, they did get more furious when being recorded while kicking off."

The fact an abuser gets angry at getting evidentially recorded indicates two things. One, they know they are behaving badly. Two, there is a real risk their bad behaviour can be shown to others, making them exposed and able to be held to account.

"Now, whenever they saw me with a recording device, they would try and grab it, call it abuse or unfair or anything they could think of to get me to stop. I didn't. And what they didn't realise was how continuously a recorder was running. On one occasion, they were being recorded kicking off on audio, chasing me up the stairs saying they were going to kill me, only to see me grab a video camera. At the thought of being recorded, they stopped and headed back downstairs saying: 'You're recording, I'll do it later.'"

This change in behaviour, when faced with it being on record, again indicates how cold-blooded abusers are. It is not a mindless rage but cold, calculated, ruthless attacks made because they think they can, and often do, get away with it.

Chapter 29

December

"Die like a dog", Abuser to Agata

3 months before escape

Letter from the Pension Service, dated 13th December 2012

...you requested a reconsideration against a decision about Pension Credit issued to you on 10/08/2012.

We have looked again at the facts and evidence we used to make our decision and looked at the points you have raised. However, we have not changed our original decision...

"Abuser had a plan to keep their mum with us long enough to pretend she was a permanent UK resident and therefore eligible for Pension Credit. It had just failed. Abuser had been banking on a lump-sum payout to clear their payday, shopping catalogue and other debts. Abuser's inspiration had been seeing people they interpreted for getting away with it and their plan had been to do the same and keep claiming even after their mother went back to Latvia. In other words, fraud."

Abuser's Diary, 22nd December 2012

Agata 00486XXXX 13.24

Mum (Victim's) Kent home 012XXXX

"Having hammered me into submission, Abuser got Agata's number and sent a burst of wrath her way too, cursing her to die like a dog, despite knowing we hadn't had an affair."

Abuser's Diary, 24th December 2012

£65 – Littlewoods catalogue

£30 – Studio

£50 – childcare

£150 – T-mobile

£300 – you need 300.

"I was paying extra for inclusive international calls from our

landline, which Abuser could easily have used at no cost to themselves. Instead they still chose to use their mobile, running up massive bills and then getting angry at the amount of money they had to pay. Instead of changing their ways, they just raged at me when it came to rent time."

Chapter 30

2013

"I'm killing you", Abuser

2 months before escape

Abuser's notice pinned on the staircase wall, 11th January 2013:

If I cry it's probably one of these

1) My children are on the SS (social services) register.

2) Victim had conspiracy with doctors behind my back.

3) Victim was beating me which caused a lump in my head (they are referring to when they hit their head on the door frame as I was dragging them off my equipment they were smashing up)

4) Victim loves reporting me to police without reason.

5) Victim betrayed me with Agata.

6) Victim was an alcoholic for 8 years.

7) Victim made fun of church and my values.

8) Victim never loved his wife.

9) Victim does not know how to feel sorry.

10) Victim tried to get rid of me and sanction me and make me lose my job and life.

11) Victim laughed at my dreams to have a ball – wedding.

12) Victim complains about me to everyone, making them believe I am mad just to destroy me.

"While Abuser was busy feeling sorry for themself, their abuse was so relentless that sometimes I still threatened to call the police. They responded with threats of more abuse."

Transcript: 1st February 2013, hallway -

ABUSER	One more word about police. Iron in your face.
VICTIM	What?
ABUSER	I'm killing you. Exactly. Stop threatening me with police. You heard me.

'Threatening' them with the police? The fact that Victim feels the need to actually record Abuser, shows just how much they feel the authorities don't listen. Given how brilliant narcissists are at lying, with both male and female abusers being able to cry on tap for sympathy, Victim is not wrong to feel this way - as what happened in October 2012 clearly demonstrated.

"Abuser made full use of the empowerment by the Crisis Team to abuse me more. They never cared if the children were there at the time. In fact they tried to involve them, to turn them against me too. *'Look kids, at this worthless, alcoholic pig.'*

The fact I was working as a long distance driver, covering over 300 miles a night, meant it would be impossible to be an alcoholic and keep any such job. Over time, as it dawned on them how ridiculous their accusations were, they changed the definition of an alcoholic, still calling me one when I had drunk two beers in two weeks. On another occasion it was after one beer in three weeks."

Transcript: 17th February 2013, 4.40pm, kitchen:

VICTIM	What?
ABUSER	Alcoholics are losers.
VICTIM	I'm not a fucking alcoholic. One drink in three weeks.
ABUSER	Stop shouting at me.
VICTIM	Fucking ridiculous.
ABUSER	Stop shouting at me.
VICTIM	I'm not shouting.
ABUSER	Good.

This is a twisting of what is generally accepted as alcoholism, a medical condition where alcohol is indeed put above other things. Abusers argument falls down in both the amount of alcohol being consumed and the lack of priority given to it. Anyone working six nights a week, in an alcohol-free role as a driver and consuming even beer a week is not, in any sense of the word, an alcoholic. Yet the word itself carries a stigma and those that hear it will assume Victim is drinking massively – potentially looking down on them and feeling sorry for Abuser. It is being used as a form of psychological abuse, to demean. Since the 'affair', they also began calling him gonorrhoea dick, for the same reason and equally untrue.

Chapter 31

DC Beth

"Beth saved our lives"

"Following the push from solicitor Caroline, I wandered into Coventry police station. The same station where PC Stuart was based and went quietly to the front desk and asked to speak to someone about domestic abuse. That was how I met DC Beth."

Extract of police log, 10 JAN 2013, 16:28:37:

VICTIM CAME IN TO THE FRONT DESK TODAY FOR SOME ADVICE. HE STATES THAT HE IS SUFFERING ONGOING VERBAL ABUSE FROM HIS WIFE AND DOES NOT KNOW WHAT TO DO. HE IS WORRIED THAT IF HE REPORTS IS SHE WILL TWIST IT ROUND AND HE WILL BE MADE OUT TO BE THE OFFENDER.

HE HAS RECORDINGS ON HIS PHONE FOF THE ABUSE.

AT THIS STAGE HE JUST WANTED ADVICE AND HE STATES HE HAS SEEN A SOLICITOR REGARDING POSSIBLE DIVORCE/CHILD CARE PROCEEDINGS....

HE SEEMED TO BE VERY DOWN TRODDEN AND STATES HE IS FINDING IT VERY HARD TO PUT UP WITH THIS ABUSE. HE STATES HE IS ALSO VERY WORRIED ABOUT MONEY BECAUSE HIS WIFE KEEPS GETTING PAY DAY LOANS AND THEY ARE STRUGGLING TO PAY THEIR DEBTS...

VICTIM STATES THEY WERE GETTING SUPPORT FROM RELATE BUT BECAUSE HIS WIFE HIT HIM WITH HER HANDBAG DURING A SESSION THEY WILL NOT SEE THEM ANY MORE.

HE SAID THAT WHEN HE WORKS NIGHTS SHE WILL NOT LET HIM SLEEP IN THE HOUSE AND HE HAS TO SLEEP IN THE CAR.

If a domestic abuse victim goes to any authority for help and is refused or exposed as having done so to their abuser, the consequences can be dire, especially when children are at risk too. Having been actively worked against by the Crisis Team and PC Stuart, this is a genuine and valid concern for Victim - now entering a potential lion's den.

"I didn't have to wait long before an interview room door opened and a female officer invited me in. There was no question of not going – the only way was forward, regardless of possible consequences."

127

Any down trodden abuse victim can feel fear of the possible consequences when walking into a police station for help. Fear of how their abuser will act when they go home and are hidden behind closed doors again. Victims can also fear the risk of having their claims turned against them, including by gender-bias.

"DC Beth was a real people person. She listened to what I had to say, also noting my body language and intonation. When I played her the recording clip, she didn't dismiss it – she agreed it was abuse. In contrast to PC Stuart, she was fully prepared to go and visit Abuser right away.Potentially to make an arrest.

'Please don't do anything yet.', **I begged. I wasn't ready with my evidence yet, needed to be certain I had enough recordings to fully evidence me as the victim, without any mass of tear-streaked lies from Abuser able to twist things against me. DC Beth understood my concerns and, before I left, gave me full assurance I would be believed and could contact her at any time. <u>DC Beth saved our lives.</u>"**

Chapter 32

The Kids and Abuser

"Paul was sitting in a chair looking miserable"

1 month before escape

"Abuser had been hammering me in bed to write an apology for my drinking and, angry at being nagged to death, I wrote one there and then, on the headboard using a black marker pen. Abuser hated this bed anyway - it was a present from my mum."

3rd February 2013, written in black marker on bed headboard

I AM REALLY SORRY FOR DRINKING FOR SO MANY YEARS

"About 5.30pm, I got home to discover Abuser had once again trashed my home office and used the same marker pen to write on our magnolia bedroom wall"

3rd February 2013, written in black marker on bedroom wall

Stop hoping that XXXX will ever love or respect you.

Their own mum does not want them so they are unable to love anyone.

"I read it then went into the boys bedroom and found Alan playing on his Wii. Paul was sitting on a chair looking miserable. I was videoing all this and, camera in hand, said: *'Paul's happy face.'* Which made him smile."

Chapter 33

One Drink Alcoholic

"And you're going to be punished", Abuser

"Abuser's favourite accusation against me was: 'alcoholic'. Perfect because they could shout it out in the street and make neighbours or anyone else listening look down on me and feel sorry for them, assuming they meant an actual alcoholic rather than someone who drank alcohol."

As we have already established, narcissists choose excuses to 'justify' their rages and, once they have found a good one they tend to stick to it as a core excuse. Others can always be added if deemed necessary. I have never heard of someone being called an alcoholic yet able to maintain a 6-night-a week job as a long-distance driver, without incident or concern from colleagues. From the transcripts, we can again see how light a drinker Victim is being.

Transcript: 17ᵗʰ February 2013, 4.28pm, kitchen -

ABUSER	I planned to go to the park but I didn't because I was too pissed off with you.
VICTIM	I'm trying to please you. Bloody hell I had one drink in three weeks
ABUSER	Kids suffered because of you.
VICTIM	One time I drink in three weeks and you kick off.
ABUSER	Your fault. XXXX your fault. I didn't make your choice. I didn't kick off anywhere. You kicked out. Don't put it as... Your fault. Purely your fault. Don't understand. OK?
VICTIM	So what have I done wrong exactly? In your eyes what have I done wrong?
ABUSER	You know how alcohol influences
VICTIM	I didn't drink in the house. I stayed outside the house.
ABUSER	It destroyed our life.
VICTIM	I stayed outside the house
ABUSER	OK you brought bad energy and demons back into our family. No it's not, fucking hell it's you. It's just you. You're the source of our loserness and bloody bad luck in this family. And

	you've been for years and years and years. And you don't see any problem with that.
VICTIM	About what? That you're calling me the source of bad luck and don't see any problem about what? What am I? So you've condemned me and I'm supposed to change something.
ABUSER	I'm not calling you, you are. You are.
VICTIM	What?
ABUSER	Alcoholics are losers.
VICTIM	I'm not a fucking alcoholic. One drink in three weeks.
ABUSER	Stop shouting at me.
VICTIM	Fucking ridiculous.
ABUSER	Stop shouting at me.
VICTIM	I'm not shouting.
ABUSER	Good.
VICTIM	Fucking hell.
ABUSER	And you're going to be punished. You're not getting away with it.
VICTIM	Getting away with what?
ABUSER	With destroying whole evening and night and morning and the whole day for kids. Only because you want to have some fun. You want to have some fun. Have some fun.
VICTIM	I had to drink alcohol outside the house. First time in 3 weeks.
ABUSER	Tough shit. You're not going to drink at all. That's my rule or you are...You're not part of my family. I'm not letting you to destroy my life. Do you understand. You already destroyed our lives

"Why would they want to give the kids a hard time because they were angry with me? Why would any parent want to do that? I didn't think it was fair not to be able to drink at all and living with their aggressions I did need to be able to unwind. By now I was feeling they didn't want me as anything more than a puppet slave, to look after the kids, provide for the family and do what ever they said I should do. It would be an existence but it wouldn't be living.

It would be psychological dominance and slavery and I was

getting ever closer to taking the recordings I had and going to DC Beth for action."

When someone has a deflection from pain as mood enhancer, whether it be alcohol, sex, gambling, sport or food, if you take that away at the same time as making their lives worse, you are putting them in a conundrum. Victim tried the compromise of going to a hotel to have a break from Abuser. And, rather than a normal person feeling guilty for driving their partner to such a measure, Abuser is enraged because they dared escape their grasp and do something they hated, associating it with the shadow of their childhood and their mother's rages at their father for drinking. What ever financial failings there were in the relationship Victim again isn't drinking enough for Abuser to complain about the money spent on alcohol; only on the cheap hotels, often just a mile down the road, to escape the rages and get some sleep. To not do what Abuser is openly trying to get them to do: crash and die, while on a long-distance night shift.

Victim's SMS, 20/02/2013, Wed 01.37

> Sorry but 99.9% have to work wed night to avoid losing job. Another reason still have it is because other agency driver gone on holiday and they couldn't cover my run for 2 weeks.

"Abuser had booked a family night for us at Legoland Windsor but I was still on a zero-hours contract and had to accept work or risk losing work. My compromise was to drive Abuser and the kids to Legoland before my shift, go to work then go back to join them in Legoland after."

Abuser's SMS, 01.46

> Don't like this.

01.53

> On top of ruining every night at home, the night for 150 pounds will also be ruined by your work. Great, especially that you sentenced me to sit in this fucking england I hate without the passport you prevented me from having. Feel sorry for myself, not you. You did not ever give a monkey about our dreams and plans anyway.

Victim's SMS, 05.15

> So while I save from your payday loans and work extra hard to keep a good job, and drive an extra 200 miles to drop you and the kids off so you

can still have fun, all you can do is complain. Complain. Complain..... Your passport issues are entirely of your making. As are your 8 months of payday loans. Home about 10am or after. Selfishly still on the road.

05.18

And petrol alone is £100, not to mention the damage to my damaged car, so don't complain about the £150 for the hotel itself.

Abuser's SMS, 08.47

My passport is your fault, payday loan would be paid off but you decided to fuck off to Agata then sanction me. So its your fault too.

Victim's SMS, 12.28

dinner almost ready. Kids too.

"I drove them all to Legoland, Windsor, stayed a little while then drove to work."

Victim's SMS, 23.26

At work but running late out of Cov.

23.29

And no money tomorrow as 150 for gas and electric comes out. Dobra noc (good night).

Abuser's SMS, 23.33

We need you more than money, come back when you can. Kids had a lot of fun wondering and exploring hotel inside out, now playing with lego game and watching tv after bath. See you soon.

23.40

Do you know at least roughly what time you will be back?

Victim's SMS, 21/02/2013, Thu, 01.11

B4 6.

Abuser's SMS, 01.16

So go straight to bed, can go for breakfast with kids before 9 and you will join in before 10. Or another option we can all go 7.30 then you will come

133

back to sleep until 10.30? Choose

After 9. Dobra noc (good night).

05.40

Arrived.

Victim and the boys, Legoland. February 2013

"We had a great family day at Legoland, then went home to 'normality' and another outburst by Abuser before I went to work again."

Abuser's SMS, 23.14

Missed call: this person/number called at 23.11 on 21st Feb but left no message.

23.20

Paul is fine, came to me and said sorry for complaining all evening. I am sorry for my part too. Its a shame that every stressful situation in our family will always be out of control because my trust and pauls nerves were needed to be damaged carelessly. Take care.

Was calling to apologize for that outburst. I was very tired and was doing my best to keep kids busy and happy, yet Paul just could not stop complaining for 2 hours. Firstly I played his game but my pieces were always wrong, then they were fighting for the sticker book, pauls pizza was apparently worse than alans so when paul started to complain about lego program which I was looking for and downloading for 40 min, I could stand only 10 min.

01.09

I still somehow love you, this is why I am so cruel about crackdown, Harry and alcohol. I am jealous.

"Very revealing sms. Abuser hates me but can't stand the idea of anyone else spending time with me, not even Harry, a male friend."

Victim's SMS, 01.37

Just got to services on m6. Thanks for smses. Suggest we go to an anger management course in birmingham. Could help us all in many ways. Kisses and goo night. Rx.

"The sweetness didn't last but still I was helping them."

Victim's SMS, 24/02/2013, Sun, 23.05

If you sign the hsbc dispute form I will fill in the rest when back and scan it so can be emailed first thing.

Abuser's SMS, 23.16

Now stop hurting my kids with your nastiness.

Projection, of the highest order.

23.17

Can you find some civilised decency in yourself and rather than torture me with your nasty game? You showed me how much you don't love me by drinking for 8 years, biting (beating) me, going to see Agata and sanctioning me. GOT THE POINT!!!!!!

Victim's SMS, 23.19

Did you write this before my hsbc sms or after

I think the same every day so it does not matter when I wrote it. What you did to me is hurting today and it will hurt tomorrow, day after tomorrow and so on.......

Victim's SMS 25/02/2013, Mon, 00.52

Thanks

Abuser's SMS 01.12

Its not a compliment, you caused a lot of pain and its not something you should be proud of.

Victim's SMS, 01.41

It was a hurt 'thanks'.

06.36

Despite you not bothering to sign the form wrote I sent hsbc dispute email for your payday loan, copy sent to you. Think will never sleep with you again after your statements about having me killed yesterday – now on sofa and from tonight on mattress topper. Tonight saved you £1000+ from your payday loan screw up. Know you will be ungrateful but did it as am a nice guy.

Abuser's SMS, 13.25

Good, your dirty dick after Agata is not an interest of mine anyway.

Victim's SMS, 13.54

House visit moved to May or later.

14.57

Hsbc got my email for you ok.

15.40

Will collect kids from after school club.

Abuser's SMS, 15.48

Chinka broke down at aldermoor. Gear box don't move at all.

"Abuser needed my help with their broken-down car so they stopped being horrible, until they got it."

Victim's SMS, 16.35

Ok. Got kids. On way.

Chapter 34

Death's Door

"Sooner or later, I would indeed crash and die"

9 days before escape

"At the time I was still a long distance driver on night shifts, typically 300 miles a night. Clean licence, never even a sniff of an alcohol issue on my record, yet Abuser still shouted I was an alcoholic and, even worse, openly stated they wanted me to crash and die every time I left for work, in front of the kids. Unbeknown to me at the time, they became terrified they would never see me again. Abuser denied me so much sleep they very nearly succeeded.

Cat naps in motorway services, gallons of coffee, singing to music, window open even in freezing temperatures. Even rubbing my genitals for emergency stimulation to avoid blacking out at the wheel. It kept me alive but was in a losing battle. By February I was so exhausted I'd wake from a 10-minute catnap in a service station, hallucinating and momentarily confused as to where I was. On the road I didn't suffer the stereo-typical nodding-off head dropping down – it was worse than that. My eyes, wide open and looking at the road ahead, simply stopped seeing. My optical brain shut down, only for moments, but this was at 70mph. When my sight came back, I would have travelled some distance, still in lane but having seen nothing during that period. It couldn't go on.

Sooner or later, I would indeed crash and die. By sheer force of will and the luck of quiet night time roads, I survived. It was only five years later, as a single parent with sole custody, that the children told me how scared they had become. Scared that when I hugged them goodbye before work, it could be the last time they saw me alive. It very nearly was."

Extract of police log, 25 FEB 2013, 17:33:57:

> VICTIM STATES TODAY THAT HIS WIFE HAS THREATENED TO TAKE THE CHILDREN OUT OF THE COUNTRY. HE HAS NOT GIVEN ME ANY DETAILS OF THE THREATS SHE IS MAKING BUT HE STATES THAT HE THINKS SHE COULD HARM HERSELF AND THE CHILDREN. ESPECIALLY IF HE TRIES TO LEAVE WITH THE KIDS.

HE HAS SAID THAT BOTH CHILDREN HAVE TOLD HIM THAT THEY WANT TO STAY WITH HIM AND THAT THEY ARE FRIGHTENED OF MUM BECAUSE SHE SHOUTS ALL OF THE TIME...

HE STATES THAT SHE HAS NOT HURT THE CHILDREN BUT THAT THEY DO WITNESS THE ARGUEMENTS. HE STATES THAT HE TRIES NOT TO ARGUE IN FRONT OF THE CHILDREN BUT THAT SHE WILL CONTINUE TO SHOUT AT HIM IF THE CHILDREN ARE PRESENT. ON SEVERAL OCCASSIONS THE CHILDREN HAVE HAD TO TELL HER TO STOP SHOUTING AT THEIR DAD.

VICTIM AGAIN STATED THAT HE HAS BEEN RECORDING THESE ARGUEMENTS AND THE THREATS SHE HAS MADE TOWARDS HIM ON HIS PHONE IN CASE HE NEEDS THEM AS EVIDENCE LATER. HOWEVER AT THIS TIME HE WILL NOT GIVE ME THE FULL DETAILS AND HAS DISCLOSED NO OFFENCES.

HE STATES THAT HE HAS BEEN TO SEE A SOLICITOR AND I HAVE ADVISED HIM TO GO BACK AND ASK ABOUT A PROHIBITED STEPS ORDER.

HE STATES SHE HAS BOOKED FLIGHTS TO TAKE THE CHILDREN OUT OF THE COUNTRY IN JULY AND HE IS WORRIED THAT SHE COULD DO SOMETHING SILLY WHILST ABROAD OR NOT RETURN THE CHILDREN. HE STATES THAT SHE HAS THE CHILDRENS PASSPORTS HIDDEN SOMEWHERE...

HE STATES THAT HE WANTS HER TO GO WITH HIM TO ANGER MANAGEMENT BUT HAS NOT YET DISCUSSED THIS WITH HER. HE FEELS THAT THIS IS THE LAST CHANCE FOR THEIR RELATIONSHIP.

HE STATES THAT HE HAS A JOB WORKING NIGHTS SO IF HE LEFT WITH THE CHILDREN HE WOULD HAVE TO GIVE UP WORK. THIS COUPLE HAVE BEEN HAVING FINANCIAL DIFFICULTIES CAUSED MAINLY BY HIS WIFE TAKING OUT PAY DAY LOANS...

HE IS CLEARLY VERY DOWN TRODDEN BY HIS WIFE AND TORN AS TO WHAT TO DO FOR THE BEST.

IT IS MY GUT FEELING THAT THERE IS A LOT MORE GOING ON HERE THAN HE IS TELLING ME. HE IS NOT TAKING POSITIVE STEPS TO DEAL WITH HIS WIFES BEHAVIOUR INCASE SHE GETS ANGRY AND IS MORE ABUSIVE TOWARDS HIM.

I HAVE ADVISED HIM THAT HE NEEDS TO PUT HIMSELF AND THE CHILDREN FIRST. I HAVE TOLD HIM HE MUST CALL THE POLICE IF SHE IS BEING THREATENING TOWARDS HIM.

PREVIOUS HISTORY:

25/11/07 VICTIM REPORTED BEING ASSAULTED BY HIS WIFE. SHE WAS ARRESTED AND ADMITTED THE ASSAULT. HE WAS NOT MAKING A FORMAL COMPLAINT SO THE MATTER WAS NFA'ED.

20/3/08 VICTIM ASSAULTED HIS WIFE. AGAIN THIS WAS NFA'ED AFTER SHE WOULD NOT MAKE A FORMAL COMPLAINT. VICTIM STATES THAT HE SNAPPED AFTER SHE VERBALLY ABUSED HIM FOR 4 HOURS.

Chapter 35

SMSes

"You made yourself to be my and kids enemy", Abuser

"Suffering relentless abuse, I had been seeing the solicitor and domestic violence officer more frequently. On this evening we took the kids to a McDonald's and in the car park I sent my mum this SMS or at least that was my intention. By mistake, I sent it to Abuser, standing nearby. I realised almost immediately but there was absolutely nothing I could do to stop it – except wait in dread for it to arrive."

Victim's SMS, 19.31, 25/02/2013 Mon

Police advised to take out prohibitive steps order so have main legal control over kids. Solicitor checking notes and will call me tomorrow. xx

"I thought they would kick off but, to my surprise, they just looked quietly annoyed and upset. After I went to work that night they sent me a message."

Abuser's SMS, 22.14, 25/02/2013 Mon

Your alcoholism and family neglect not to mention physical abuse caused my depression nothing else and stop pretending that you are a victim and my mental health is nothing to do with you. You are such a terrible husband that its really better to be dead than keep suffering being married to you.

Victim's SMS 22.16

I have changed. Why can't you?

22.53

And I do care about you.

Abuser's SMS, 03.13, 26/02/2013 Tue

Do you mean changed from being an alcoholic to being a nasty traitor? Wow!!

03.23

You showed 1000 times how much you did not care about me and kids in the past. Its too late for me to have any trust in you and give you chances. You damaged everything which is possible to damage. If you woke up earlier, like couple of years ago. Now I refuse to believe in you. You made

141

yourself to be my and kids enemy, enemy I used to love.

03.27

Keep up with your threats and sleep on sofa downstairs as you decided last night. Don't care any more. You wanted to break our marriage – you succeeded, congratulations.

Victim's SMS, 03.32

Sleep. Wish I could.

Abuser, SMS, 04.32

Are you tired of fighting and decided to be a nice guy until you will get stronger and will be releasing your poison on me again? Had enough of this cycle. Fuck off.

"When I got home after my night shift the door was locked, key in it. I don't remember if I slept in the car or a hotel."

Abuser's SMS, 11.56

Since October I can't sleep, you devil took my sleep. I hope Agata was worth it, that your family life is ruined now and I have no desire to trust you to build with anything. You are out. Come back to Agata.

"Knowing there was never any resolution to their false accusations, my reply ignored their comments."

Victim SMS, 11.59

We can tow Cinque home or to a scrapyard but guess it needs to be today.

"The clutch had gone on their Fiat Cinquecento so was trying to be pragmatic as they needed a car for work. No reply so wrote again."

Victim's SMS, 14.19

In town to talk to bank about my loan. Want to meet?

15.02

Found you a possible car in CV4, a Renault Clio, 07759xxxxx

15.11

Toyota Corolla in Birmingham too. Both on ebay.

"Still no reply but knew they were finishing work so sent another."

Want a lift?

"They finally replied."

Abuser's SMS, 17.25

By not giving me Agata's number you showed very clearly what you stand for in life. Will be taking drugs, will show kids how to take them and you can start begging me now to stop as it might take a while (more like 8 years) before I will want to listen to you.

Victim's SMS, 00.09, 27/02/2013 Wed

March 16th free day for me to book something for family day?

05.30

Got home early at 4.20am and locked out, again! Was knocking on door and ringing phone for 20 mins. Angry.

Abuser's SMS, 08.06

Go to Agata or your mums place perhaps? The woman you ignored and disrespected for so many years does not give a monkey any more.

Victim, SMS, 08.06

Stop fucking about with our home!!!!

Abuser, SMS, 08.07

Alternatively call police or Dr Gillian, they are closer to your heart than your family, traitor. Want a separation.

Victim, SMS, 08.07

STOP FUCKING ABOUT WITH OUR HOME!!!

Abuser's SMS, 08.13

Stop fucking about with everything, I don't want you unconditionally. You chose alcohol, Agata, your films over your family and here is the natural follow up – I am not pleased with your choice. What happened to Harry's place? Or is it for the special times to piss me off not when you really need it. Had enough of you. Separation please.

Victim's SMS, 08.15

Home in 5. No more shit. If you don't open the door everything recorded goes straight to the police. Your choice.

Call the crisis team too. You need help, perhaps they can assess you quicker since you are so distressed, and stop pestering me. I don't want you. You wasted every single chance was given to you, now you can fuck off.

08.24

You did not build a home, you were ruining what I was trying to build so there is nothing to come back to for you now. Go to your mums and live with dogs. I will have another 2 children, but not with you.

08.33

You took my passport, so I can't run away from you, well it gives me no choice but hate you.

"I had hidden Abuser's passport because they had threatened to take our children abroad and vanish, possibly kill them. From phone records, two places they was considering were confirmed as Russia and Dubai. Neither have a reciprocal return agreement with the UK."

Chapter 36

Five Days to Arrest

"Yes, that's sad, I'm bullying you", Abuser

5 days before escape

1st March

"It was about 6.30pm. Abuser and I were sitting at the dining room table eating soup and discussing when they would need lifts after my night shift. Alan kept interrupting to show me the Star Wars 'Angry Birds' he was playing on my phone – in flight mode as I was against Wi-Fi and phone radiation for children on safety grounds. I had a video camera recording through a glass-fronted cabinet and it looks like a pleasant family scene, with Abuser even smiling at times. The topic of bullying at school came up, not involving our boys but their friends. On that topic Abuser then made a comment about us."

Transcript: 1st March 2013, 6pm, dining room -

ABUSER	Bullying is something... I'm bullying you. I'm doing this deliberately... Yes, that's sad, I'm bullying you... There are so many psychological aspects for this... I personally think bullying... I, a person with a masters degree (in teaching)... You should never apply 'bullying' to people as young as 7,8,9,10... You can talk about bullying when people are mature....
	Alan, there is no problem if there is no victim... Don't agree to be a victim...
VICTIM	So then how come I am a victim?
ABUSER	You're not a victim.
VICTIM	I am.
ABUSER	Well, because I don't want you to make me a victim.

Chapter 37

Three Days to Arrest

"I will destroy you", Abuser

3 days before escape

3rd March

Transcript: 3rd March 2013, 2.39am, in bed -

| ABUSER | Just remember you will never succeed with your books. Never. Never with your films. You're cursed just like your mum. Never… You will never publish anything. You will never get any employment. Just rip your future dreams and put them in your fat arse. Even if you will, I will destroy your future. That's my mission. You destroyed mine, I will be destroying yours. |

"It didn't matter how much I tried to appease Abuser or keep trying to go forward despite suffering their abuse – they were never happy, always angry. How had I destroyed their dreams? What dreams was I supposed to have destroyed? Dancing on my grave? They never said. As far as I could tell, it was just another accusation to throw at me, to 'justify' how badly they treated me.

Later that night they physically kicked me out of bed and told me to sleep on the sofa. Angry, I went downstairs and grabbed a can of beer. Knowing Abuser's pattern would be to follow me, to attack me more, I also set up a video camera to record it. Minutes later, down they came."

Transcript: 3rd March, 3.37am, living room to sleep on sofa -

ABUSER	And you're not going to London. I will destroy you. Do anything. Destroy by any means.
VICTIM	You don't want me to get this job?
ABUSER	I don't give a shit about your work, you'll be destroyed. Understand. Completely destroyed as you destroyed me. I can't go to our medical centre now. I have three assignments I'm absolutely dreading now. All I can think is what I'm going to say to Dr Gillian when I will see her. Hello nasty doctor… I can smell alcohol.

VICTIM	One can.
ABUSER	In your fucking face. I told you off what I think about alcohol.
VICTIM	It's because you started hitting me in bed.
ABUSER	So get out to Harry's place then. You're not drinking under this roof.
VICTIM	That's the last one. I don't have any more.
ABUSER	I don't believe you.
VICTIM	I'm just sitting on this fucking sofa
ABUSER	Yes I felt you would be drinking downstairs
VICTIM	I knew you would come. I was waiting for you.
ABUSER	Yes so you decided to drink. You will be sleeping here another day and another day. It's what you want, yes?
VICTIM	Abuser, it's just one beer.
ABUSER	You started. You started by drinking.
VICTIM	No you started by hitting me in bed.
ABUSER	You started by drinking. You started by drinking. And my reaction always will be the same. Understand. And now I'll be kicking off until Monday because you drank that one. I'll never permit alcohol under this roof. Never. Over my dead body you'll need to kill me before drinking. I've had enough of you in my life with your stupid drinking and your stupid attitude You're pushing too far.
VICTIM	I'm pushing too far?
ABUSER	Fucking pushing too far. You're really pushing too far. You should say thank you I didn't start smoking today in front of everyone and instead of appreciating this what's he doing? He's getting another beer.
VICTIM	I bought four, I drank three earlier.
ABUSER	I don't care how many you bought. It's like this stupid explanation I bought ticket it's why I went to Krakow. Oh I bought beers so I need to drink them.
VICTIM	XXXX I...

ABUSER	Oh I bought drugs it's why I need to smoke them.
	I have no life and you have no life. You damaged me. You damaged my brain. Sadist. If you stopped drinking five years ago it would be fixable. Wasn't that damaged. And still somehow I felt something to you. Now you decided to push it whole hog until there is nothing come back. And what were you thinking with one beer?

"They then grabbed the almost full can and poured it over me. I just felt glad when they left, knowing they were unlikely to return and that a camera had been recording how they chose to be. Chose to be. Nobody forced them to be abusive except themself.

As always, as the next day dawned, they denied any wrong doing and that afternoon told me I had gone to sleep on the sofa simply because I wanted to."

Chapter 38

4th March 2013

"Yes, I want to be in charge", Abuser

2 days before escape

"Looking at these transcripts, I don't even remember why Abuser wanted to call my brother, Damien, but remember the abuse of the situations themselves very well and the fact I was refusing to give his number to avoid them sending him abuse too. The whole thing still sickens me."

Transcript: 4th March 2013, 12.05pm, kitchen -

VICTIM	If you want we can call him this evening. Damien.
ABUSER	Do you understand what harm you're doing? Do you understand what harm you are doing instantly now. It reminds me of what you were doing with Agata. It reminds me of every time you were blackmailing me. ...you're allowed to talk behind my back. You want... Asking for help but you still can't help it. The call to Damien keeps me sane! You idiot. You don't understand at all psychology, you fucking piece of shit.
VICTIM	What..? What would you say to Damien? Don't fucking hit me.
ABUSER	I'm going to hit you. I'm going to hit you. Give me fucking number of Damien.
VICTIM	No
ABUSER	Give me number of Damien.
VICTIM	Stop hitting me. Stop hitting me!
ABUSER	Give me the number of Damien.
VICTIM	One more time and I'm calling the police. Right, that's it.
ABUSER	Give me fucking number of Damien.
VICTIM	No!
ABUSER	(spits)

VICTIM	Bitch.
ABUSER	Piece of shit. All fucking shit.

"I left the house, to get a break in a cafe, returning a few hours later."

Transcript: 4th March 2013, 4.15pm, kitchen -

ABUSER	Don't you get it. There is nothing to explore. All borders been crossed. The next time it's just me jumping with kids and dying. And it's not a threat any more it's a statement. Because I'll do this. If not this summer next summer. If not next summer in two years' time. I swear on God.
ABUSER	And finally my soul will go and be with someone I love. Because in real life I can't be with you. I'm fed up by fucking snakes like you. Snakes who go to Ikea when I'm in distress.
VICTIM	You told me get out.
ABUSER	And sit there drinking coffee and making plans and making calls probably to your mum.
VICTIM	You were invited.
ABUSER	I don't want to go to Ikea. Why did you leave me in distress?
VICTIM	You told me to get out
ABUSER	Nothing of this would happen. It's your fault. Do you understand? Piece of shit it's your fault. I needed to destroy something. Every time you're leaving me I have an urge to destroy something.
VICTIM	Why did you tell me to get out?
ABUSER	I can't get out.
VICTIM	No. Why did you tell me to get out?
ABUSER	I'm depressed.
VICTIM	Why did you tell me to get out?
ABUSER	Because I knew that you were going to go out and bloody in out in out in out. I have this fucking...
VICTIM	So why tell me to go then complain that I went out?
ABUSER	Because you were on your way anyway.

150

VICTIM	Are you just trying to be in charge?
ABUSER	You you would get out anyway. Yes I want to be in charge. And this number that would be some kind of giving me this responsibility because you are fucking control freak. You just want to keep everything. My passport, kids, you're not allowed to leave the country. I've got your passport I've got everything, nationality da de da da. I hate this. Do you understand? I hate.
VICTIM	You've got the kids passports.
ABUSER	I can't leave them. Well now you're pushing I'll probably need to send them with someone else 'cause I have no choice. Do you understand. I have no choice. You are pushing me into this. I wouldn't have done this but now I need to send kids to someone else abroad. Because you piece of shit took my passport.
	CLIP ENDS
Footnote	Abuser had their passport, not Victim.

"In Latvia, Abuser's parents lived in a 12th floor flat. This is the place they were talking about jumping from with the kids. They later denied it, again, but had not just said but sworn to God they would take the kids there and kill them. At other times they specified they would drug the kids first, before jumping with them to go to a 'better life'. And then attack me for taking their passports.

They are complaining of me taking their passports here, yet they have them. Forcibly demanded back in October, five months earlier - after being empowered by the Crisis Team, who logged Abuser as the victim and me as the abuser. Abuser also had their own passport.

This was all just part of the usual recycling of old events and never going forward. Never enjoying any positives or even seeming to want them. As far as I could tell, they didn't want any solutions to anything – just wanted to complain. Endlessly complain about me and everyone else who dared not to agree with everything they said or did."

151

Chapter 39

5th March 2013

alcohol assessment unit

1 day before escape

"Still trying to keep Abuser happy, I agreed to go to the local drug and alcohol addicts centre to be assessed. Seeing Abuser standing next to me and doing all the talking to book me in, they asked if I was there by my own choice or because had been forced to be there. I said they had forced me to be there – to which their response was to deny Abuser's presence during the assessment, which they had to accept.

In the assessment, the female worker was very balanced and professional. I told her what I drank, how often and why. Unlike Abuser saying alcoholism had nothing to do with the amount of alcohol consumed, according to this professional it did. She also realised I wasn't dependent, was a stable, normal and hard-working father in a difficult marriage.

Having met Abuser, albeit briefly, she asked what support networks were in place and I explained about the Crisis Team, having the contact with the police domestic violence unit and that had been recording Abuser to evidence the abuse. She wished me luck and I left, deemed not to an alcoholic.

When I got home Abuser was a little subdued. Their plan to embarrass me in front of officials had back-fired, for the official for alcoholics had affirmed I was not one and that Abuser was wrong about this. The peace didn't last because, with narcissists, it never does.

I went to my driving job that night and, despite all the rubbish and hell with Abuser, felt positive because the next morning I had an interview for more TV work, this time not Channel 4 for a documentary for National Geographic. Or so I thought..."

Chapter 40

Arrested and Charged

"I'm killing myself and kids", Abuser

6th March 2013

"I had only got to bed about 6.30am after my night shift, to grab a few hours sleep before going to London for the interview, when Abuser awoke me early, at school time."

These transcripts and recording clips are not yet complete but complete enough to give you the idea – bold indicates the start of sections.

Transcript, 6th March 2013, 8.30am -

	SOUND OF A DISTURBANCE
ABUSER	**This is deliberate.**
VICTIM	What?
ABUSER	So you can't sleep normally before your interview. You fucking failed.
ABUSER	Was Agata worth it? Piece of shit. Well was she? You still didn't answer my question which I wrote on our wedding photo. Was she. XXXX was. Was it so difficult to give her number. I needed to be sanctioned because you couldn't give her number. XXXX You don't respect. You don't love. What do you give to other people XXXX zero. In October did you actually offer any solutions did you offer like: Abuser I love you very much perhaps lets call to Agata together and talk to her. Never.
VICTIM	You spoke to Agata.
ABUSER	Instead let's play this game this dodgy game. I will call her. Don't move don't XXXX come lets hate and mistrust you my wife. I will call this darling Agata. Glorified. On the top of my list. You can go and sleep at her place if you want to rest now. You put me down so much. Humiliated me so much. I have nothing XXXX. Nothing left in my life. XXXX
ABUSER	I wish you're not back ever from London. I mean it. and mean it and mean it. XXXX. You can go straight through to your mum (in Kent) or fly XXXX to Agata. You made your choice. It was very clear. Or what don't you understand of what I've said when

	I told there is no space for me and Agata in your life. XXXX in our family. You still dared 'oh she kissed me she's fine' so let's call my mum now. XXXX it's my mum. It's my mum. Don't need your help any more
ALAN	**Mummy what's our excuse for missing school. Oh sorry my mum's shouting at my dad.**
ABUSER	Dad was fucking with Agata
ALAN	Not my dad. No my mum XXXX
ALAN & PAUL	(Talking outside bedroom) XXXX
ABUSER	Daddy loves us. XXXX yeah. Ruined family. Ruined psychology of kids XXXX. 2008 I was asking you Rich I'm about to cross the border of my patience. What did you do. Nothing. He was still fighting for his right to drink. Every single time I would beg him I would tell him I would get hysteria he was just 'ha ha ha She's mentally ill. Ha' That's why she's having hysteria. No because I'm intelligent enough to see where it goes when people are living when people have no trust and love this is XXXX how life looks like. I knew about this two or three years ago. You a rotten head can't predict things. He's working for National Geographic XXXX can't predict his own family events. He can work for National Geographic. They taking piss or what. Nobody will give you employment XXXX and loser.

The children were watched safely crossing the road by both parents and now safely at school, 200m away. Back in the home, Abuser continued having a go at Victim in the bedroom. Then followed them into the bathroom.

Transcript, 6th March 2013, 9am - bathroom -

ABUSER	**OK. It can't get any worse but I'll try my best. OK. I'll start killing myself and kids, then probably you'll see the effects. Yes? Better? Then you'll be on your knees and saying sorry? When? Tell me what is your breaking point? Never happens.**
VICTIM	XXXX...
ABUSER	You're such a piece of shit. Tell me are you such a piece of shit that you can't just feel sorry? Tell me, can you feel sorry

	generally in your life? Can you?
VICTIM	I'm very sorry.
ABUSER	That's not enough on your knees, I told you.
VICTIM	No, because you spit at me
ABUSER	OK I'm killing myself and kids because it's the only way with you. You are piece of shit. You see you are piece of shit. Feeling sorry is actually something normal people... People who are brave. People with heart can do. How I was... it's taken all these years... I'm making to feel better. 'Ryszku Pyszku' was made up – was a made up character. I'm adapting with my big heart (for) this person because I've made you to be something you've never been. I gave you this characteristic you never had. And this is real you now in front of me. A person who can't feel sorry. Who can stab and kill his whole family. And he can't find the sorrow. And even when I'm asking for this. It's not that you... It's bad enough that you don't have it naturally, you don't have it even when you're asked.
	VICTIM STARTS THE SHOWER, WHICH REQUIRES KNEELING DOWN TO AVOID WATER SPLASHING.
ABUSER	Oh gosh. You're such a piece of shit you can't feel pain. People like you should just be left and I should run away from you. Come on wash your gonorrhoea dick.
VICTIM	Why did you send me a text to say: 'until Friday'?
ABUSER	I'll explain when you... because you can't say sorry is XXXX Same reason I kissed you. Well, I let you kiss me. Ah you always can kiss me, I don't care. It's all a delusion for the kids, but you're not having me. My lovely pussy will belong to any man who wants me, not you. Understand and it will be loved and treasured and appreciated, not a piece of shit who can't even say sorry after fucking betraying me. And leaving me in misery. Keep leaving me in misery. You are, your choice
ABUSER	And my attempts to make your choice, to change your choices, it's just like you know. It's just like hitting myself against the wall.
	VICTIM'S SHOWER RESUMES
ABUSER	And you can't even let me go to Latvia where I have support, yeah? I'm dying here. My closest person doesn't choose to help me. And just stabbing me. Keep, keep stabbing me. And my

	kids is what it means, because when I'm going down my kids are going down. Don't you see? Every time I'm shouting what affect it has on them.
VICTIM	I know that.
ABUSER	And you make me shouting. You make me shouting so why you fucking don't stop doing it?
VICTIM	Abuser I'm not doing anything. I was bloody at work last night.
ABUSER	I'll kill you. That's it. Today's the day. I can't stand you any more
VICTIM	I'm taking a shower.
ABUSER	I want to just hear sorry, nothing else.
VICTIM	I'm sorry.
ABUSER	It's not enough, because I asked you for this.
VICTIM	So when. When am I supposed to say it?
ABUSER	When I was here. When I was here, when I told you on your knees and say sorry, you said 'no'.
VICTIM	I did say sorry.
ABUSER	Why did you fuck say no? One more time...
	ABUSER GRABS GLASS DOLPHIN AND RAISES IT ABOVE VICTIM'S HEAD – AS THEY ARE KNEELING IN THE BATH. VICTIM FEARS FOR THEIR SAFETY AND MAKES A GRAB FOR IT. A STRUGGLE ENSUES.
ABUSER	What are you fucking doing?
VICTIM	What do you think you're doing?
ABUSER	What do you fucking doing? I'm fucking...
VICTIM	Get away from me.
ABUSER	Never. No.
VICTIM	Get the fuck away from me.
ABUSER	No. No. That's your no. No. It's a man who can say sorry, gonorrhoea dick.
VICTIM	Get the fuck away from me.
ABUSER	No.

VICTIM	Get out this bathroom.
ABUSER	No. You killed me. You can't kill me again. You can butcher me as much as you want you can't kill me. Because you killed my love already.
	ABUSER HAS BEEN REPEATEDLY TRYING TO HIT VICTIM IN THE FACE WITH THE GLASS DOLPHIN. WET FROM THE SHOWER VICTIM IS LOSING GRIP AND KICKS THEM ONCE, IN THE BELLY, MAKING THEM DROP IT.
ABUSER	And you kicked me, in the belly.
VICTIM	And the dolphin you were trying to throw at me?
ABUSER	You kicked me in the belly. This is what instead of saying sorry but you're...
VICTIM	I said sorry, you still kept on.
ABUSER	You didn't say sorry, I pushed you into this - it doesn't count. You're not generally sorry. Parasite. So what? So what? You've killed the woman in front of you. You killed and murdered. So what? Dirty moron. And I give you so many chances. He's kicking them all. And I will kill you if you come back, so stay in London forever.
VICTIM	You just tried to kill me now.
ABUSER	Yes. And you tried to kill me too.
VICTIM	Then why aren't you dead?
ABUSER	So why are you not dead?
VICTIM	Because I defended myself.
ABUSER	No. No, no, no, no because I didn't attack you. I had this very close to you and I could get into your eye if I wanted to kill you, within a second.
VICTIM	You think I'm actually going to wait for you to swing at my head, yeah?
ABUSER	No you didn't wait. I didn't do this.
VICTIM	You were bloody one foot away from my face.
ABUSER	No, no, no you don't appreciate how quickly I can do it. And I didn't do this. This is the thing. I was just playing with you.
VICTIM	No. It's not a game, Abuser.

157

ABUSER	Well, it is a game for you. No... Fucking Agata, such a lovely game. And later blaming everyone. Such a fantastic man. And must enjoy... I'll be killing you every day now.
VICTIM	You broke my watch as well (in the bathroom struggle).
ABUSER	I will be killing you every day. Hah, hah, hah, had. Yes. And other equipment and crap...
ABUSER	You exchange me for equipment, for Agata, for your mum so everything will be dying out – piece by piece in your life. Because I'm dead already. You killed me. Well good, yes, so I'll have a bruise.
VICTIM	Abuser I've got a cut on my arm.
ABUSER	I'll go to police...
VICTIM	So go.
ABUSER	Oh, so go? This is how much you care, yeah? This is to show how you show how much you care: 'So go'.
	VICTIM GOES TO RESUME SHOWER. ABUSER CONTINUES ESCALATING.
VICTIM	Don't start again.
ABUSER	I will. I will. I will. As much as it fucking takes. You're not having a shower
VICTIM	Get out of this room.
ABUSER	No
VICTIM	Get out of this room.
ABUSER	No.
VICTIM	Get out of this room
ABUSER	(spits) No.
VICTIM	Fucking bitch
ABUSER	No. Why would I? It's my house?
VICTIM	You want to push me to the point, yeah?
ABUSER	What? You pushed it to the very point already. You know that you pushed it. You killed me. You eventually killed me. You already was trying to kill me in 2008 and this is again. As if I don't know you. I will trigger you right back after this. Piece of shit. Piece of shit. No. I need that.

158

VICTIM	Get out.
	ANOTHER STRUGGLE - VICTIM FORCES ABUSER OUT OF THE BATHROOM. THEY COME BACK IN.
ABUSER	OK.
	VICTIM FORCES THEM OUT AGAIN AND INTO THE BEDROOM, TEMPORARILY RESTRAINING THEM ON THE BED
ABUSER	You're not fucking.. You piece of shit...
VICTIM	Listen, You stop this.
ABUSER	Fuck.
VICTIM	You stop this. Fuck.
ABUSER	So fuck off from my life then.
VICTIM	Stop this.
ABUSER	Fuck off from my life then. Fuck off from my life. Never come back from Agata. Understand? I will come back, piece of parasite. Never come back.
VICTIM	Stops today. It stops today.
ABUSER	(spits) Get off (out). Go and fuck Agata. Go and fuck...
VICTIM	You want to go again?
ABUSER	Yes... Kill me...
	ANOTHER STRUGGLE
ABUSER	Come on. I'm not afraid. You think I'm afraid to die? Piece of shit.
	VICTIM RETURNS TO BATHROOM TO FINISH SHOWER
VICTIM	Mad.
	ABUSER COMES AFTER THEM
ABUSER	He prefers to beat his wife instead of saying on knees and saying sorry. It shows your devil face who never loved... Fine. Come on beat me more. What else can you do? Next stop beat your children for something... Crap. You piece of shit. Been trying to protect from you, kids all of my life. And I'm still looking for National Geographic number (Victim has an interview for them that morning), so I'll call

everywhere. Fucking piss your life down.

They will know what crap of shit you are too. Everyone will tell you... put you into jail in this country. So everybody won't (work with you) ...the exact situation. Many people on this side. A fucking alcoholical liar, who said the assessment was nothing (the forced visit, by Abuser, to a medical centre that assessed Victim was not an alcoholic – which Abuser is angry about) You just lied and I told this woman too. Not alcoholic... Hah, hah. And she probably knows it from your appearance . The same with drug takers. Yes they'll come to you and tell you exactly how much they take? Ahah? Yeah. In my dream.... what do you expect from alcoholic? You never take responsibility that you ruined the life, with alcohol, of his family. And never. And remember Rich, it will get worse if you come back so better not to. I will be killing you everyday now. Every single day. This is how far you pushed me, you piece of shit. It will be your last chance. To get on your knees everyday and say sorry. No he can't do this. He prefers to keep killing. And it's the only solution and you're not taking it. So I have... I'm left with nothing. Since you killed me and you don't want to admit this and feel sorrow, the only way is to revenge and kill you back.

I'll be attempting to murder you every day. Do you understand? Every single day. As a matter of fact I'm waiting when you will go on the stairs and I will push you...

"And this is the poor, supposedly scared little woman the Crisis Team supported against 'abuser' me."

The way in which Abuser is talking shows they are not looking for any solutions. If Victim says sorry, they say it doesn't count because they made them do it. If they don't say sorry they says they don't care so have to say sorry. When Victim did say sorry Abuser spat in their face. All they are trying to do is to put them down.

The fact Abuser is failing to emotionally make them submit, is infuriating for them so they up the game, bringing in physical violence, threats of belittling to others, ruining their career and death threats. Abuser's 'justification' for this is everything they can think of from the past: their arrest in 2008, their claim of an affair - previously admitted as knowing it never happened - and even their imposed alcohol assessment, which didn't get the the result they wanted.

In terms of the physical violence, on one hand they are saying how easily they could have blinded Victim and on the other saying Victim was wrong to grab for the weapon held above their face. At no point do they even attempt to reign themself in and think, *'Hang on a moment, this is all ridiculous. What I am saying makes no sense.'* Instead, with Victim's refusal to break down, Abuser continues – still telling them it is all their fault.

Transcript, 6th March 2013, 9.20am -

ABUSER	They (the children) don't come from your body they come from my body. And you just exercising tortures on this link non-stop. 'She wanted to kill and da de da'. You don't understand that killing, the word kill, comes from the pain that you are torturing me so much over years and years with your drinking that I'm eventually dead and all that I can want is just to change my body. And kids won't be happy without me so if I will die kids will follow me.
ABUSER	And instead of doing something to make me happy what did you do to make me happy. What. What exactly did you do to make me happy, ever.
VICTIM	Nothing it seems. According to you.

Transcript, 6th March 2013, 9.23am -

VICTIM	What have I done since I've come back from work, apart from sleep? What?
ABUSER	You don't know?
VICTIM	Apparently yes so explain to me.
ABUSER	Idiot, you are stupid so explanation won't help. I'm going somewhere else. OK. Me and kids are going somewhere else. Different world. In a world you'll never find us. You'll be in your alcoholic world. I will be in my world. So run away. Chop chop.
	GAP AS VICTIM GOES TO GET READY FOR LONDON JOB INTERVIEW
ABUSER	You're causing so much...
VICTIM	What?
ABUSER	You're causing so much pain in my life.
VICTIM	I'm just going to bloody work, Abuser.
ABUSER	No. It's not that easy. It's not that easy. Stop making innocent. You're a bloody devil who can't apologise. A woman who

	come to you asking you to get on your knees. You prefer to punch me, kick me rather than get on your knees.
VICTIM	**You came at me with that glass dolphin.**
ABUSER	And I will be hitting you until you get on your knees and if you will never get on your knees me and kids will be drugged forever. Do you understand? Because I can't live in this torture of your not being sorry. And looking at me as an innocent angel. You're a fucking devil. Do you understand? You're devil. Piece of shit devil.
ABUSER	You're not a nice person. You never been. I made you to be nice because I have a very big heart. Making you to look nice in front of other people when you really are...
ABUSER	And you want to show off in front of... you piece of shit. I should have seen it earlier. How you treat your sisters, your mother. Keeping hands off your mother not because you respect her but... you do everything to piss me off. And I had enough of this torture, of your pissing me off by your action. By your... As if seem to be innocent action and that's it. I'm running away in a very specific way and I'm not telling you what way. You will never find me. Never. Do you understand? Neither kids...
ABUSER	I told you, you're pushing me too far. You saw that I was bloody... they knew me at CDT (the assessment centre). I'm just dying. I have access to any drugs I want. Blackmailing to you. I just need to find out what dosage to stop life for kids, to hook them for life. For me I love my kids and I don't want them to go through what I am going through and I see Paul is coming there. He will not stand your sadist nature. Nobody can stand your sadism. The only way is to fucking go XXXX from you because in that state nobody will care about your sadism. XXXX you eventually XXXX your family. Piece of shit.

Even Abuser could see that Paul was 'coming there', by which they mean becoming angry like them. The thing they fail to take on board is Paul is only becoming like them because of how they choose to be. If Abuser really loves their children, why do they not change their behaviour?

The only torturing being done here, as the transcripts illustrate, is by Abuser. The same goes for sadism and abuse; this too all comes from them, projected upon Victim for they remain unable to face the fact it is all inside them. Their issue.

"All their abuse was nothing new. Not the physical attacks, not the demeaning controlling behaviour, not the threats of more abuse or even the endless spiteful lies. I still opened the front door, barely slept after my night shift, to go not to the police but to London for my interview. Then Abuser, wanting to give me a final kick on the way out, came to the front door as I was closing it and pulled it back open."

In 2007, Abuser was arrested for attacking Victim out of anger. In 2008, after 4 hours of escalating physical, verbal and psychological abuse, Victim snapped and assaulted them back, also arrested. No charges were brought in either case. Then, in 2012, after major escalations and threats to kill the kids, Victim went to their GP for help, who referred matters to the Crisis Team, which Abuser turned against them to the point they were preparing sole custody for Abuser. This gave official empowerment to the real abuser and they took full advantage of it, weaponising the kids lives against Victim.

Transcript: 22ⁿᵈ November 2012, 4.07am, in bed -

ABUSER	It's better to kill myself and children than let children to live without me. So if you will ever attempt to separate me with children yes I will kill all of us.

These further threats to kill the children add a specific condition upon which Abuser would do so, combined with their description of how they would do it.

Transcript: 4ᵗʰ March 2013, 4.15pm, kitchen -

ABUSER	Don't you get it. There is nothing to explore. All borders been crossed. The next time it's just me jumping with kids and dying. And it's not a threat any more it's a statement. Because I'll do this. If not this summer next summer. If not next summer in two years' time. I swear on God.

Yet on this day, 6ᵗʰ March 2013, even after being attacked twice in the bathroom, with all the verbal and psychological abuse launched on top, Victim has still contained themself. Abuser, obviously not satisfied with the level of hurt given, decides that only further poison will do. They, once again, go after them with another put down. This is the put down that changed the course of their history, for it forced the response Victim had been avoiding.

"I looked at Abuser, standing ever angry in the doorway, holding it as if poised to slam it in my face. Out of everything else they told me then, the words that stuck were the words that shaped what happened next: *'When you get back from London,*

me and the kids will be gone.' As those words began sinking in I said nothing back - just looked at them as they closed the door.

For a moment, I just stood there, processing how they had just given me no choice but formal action. I had stayed in that hell house to safeguard the kids and they had just told me they were going to vanish them, with all their stated threats of murdering them when they did so. My London interview was meaningless compared to the kids' safety.

I got in my car in the drive but didn't start the engine. Instead I picked up the phone and called the National Geographic TV company to apologise for not being able to make the interview. As I was on the phone, Abuser came out of the house – giving no sign they saw me sitting there. I watched to see which way they would go. Towards the school or the other way. Thankfully, at the end of the drive they turned right, away from the school. I didn't have to race them there. I could get there first without a fight, for this was the stage we were at now. War. The greatest battle for the safety of the children, against the person who should have been their greatest protector but was instead their greatest threat – their mother."

With that call, Victim demonstrates exactly who they put first: the children. Forced to put their faith back in the system, they make a second call.

"Like a robot on autopilot, I then called DC Beth, telling her I had just been attacked by Abuser, that they had threatened to vanish the kids today and that I was now going to the school to protect them. DC Beth, the officer who had repeatedly assured me my side would be fairly listened to, did not let us down. As good as her word, she told me to wait at the school and officers would come to meet me there.

If there had been any time to think of myself, I would probably have cried with relief. Thinking of myself was a luxury that had been devoid for many years. My kids needed me and to their school I went, to make sure Abuser couldn't take them and to wait for the police to arrive. It was my duty to protect the children from our abuser and that was the entire focus of what I did."

Police Report, 10:47 hours Wed 6th March 2013

Offence Code: 0F61102

Description: WOU 47 ASSAULT OCCASSIONING ABH

Offence Times: Between 09.30 hours Wed 6th Mar 2013 and 10:47 hours Wed 6th Mar 2013.

WEAPON TYPES – USAGE: OTHERS – USED AS A THREAT

MODUS OPERANDI & PROPERTY:

BMT IP AND OFFENDER HAVE HAD A VERBAL ALTERCATION AT THE LOCATION. DURING THE ALTERCATION THE OFFENDER HAS TAKEN A DOLPHIN ORNAMANENT FROM THE SIDE AND HAS THREATENED THE IP WITH IT. THE IP HAS ATTEMPTED TO GET THE ORNAMENT FROM THE OFFENDER AND THERE HAS BEEN A STRUGGLE.... DV RISK MEDIUM.

"Believing I wouldn't be recording in the bathroom, when arrested Abuser lied I was the one who had attacked them. My recordings demonstrated otherwise. Even the arresting officers found their behaviour so bad they put in a complaint against them.

Years later, now a music teacher for young teenagers back in Latvia, Abuser still tells everyone they are the victim. That I, as an English bastard, set them up."

Epilogue

2013 to 2025

2013

"At 4.30am, Abuser got into my car as I parked after a night shift and spent 3 hours apologising then seducing me. Remember, sex was the best thing between us and I still loved them. I wouldn't break the court order banning them from entering our home so both drove to their nephew's place, snuck into the room where they were staying and fucked. Maybe things could work out between us?

Turned out their aim was another pregnancy, as a new hook, and when that didn't happen, they claimed it was rape – forgetting they had sent happy, loving thank you messages afterwards. Presented with these, the police dropped the case but did they take action against Abuser for demonstrably lying? Of course not."

A few weeks later, organised by Abuser's brother and sister, Victim met them and Abuser to talk about possible ways forward. This injury was the result, photographed the day after – a dozen stitches in their lip.

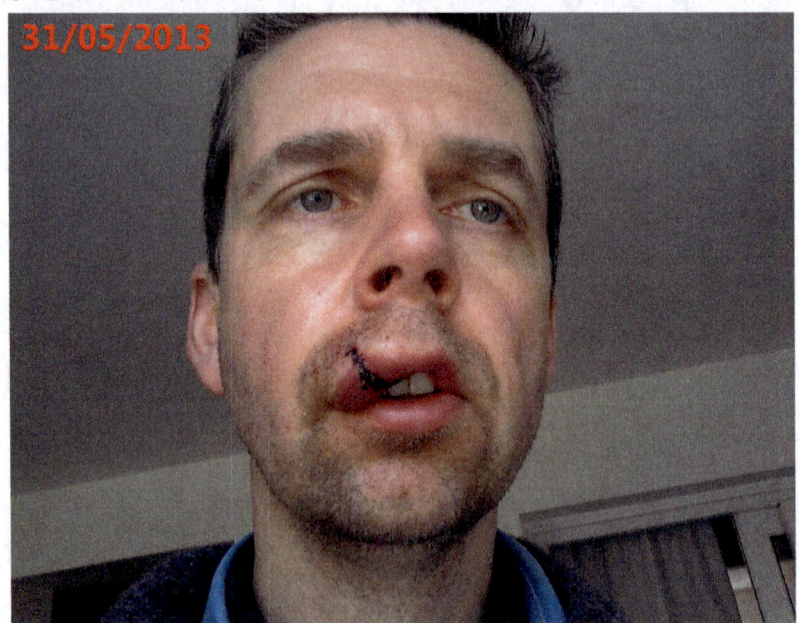

Victim after meeting Abuser to try and reconcile contact. May 2013

"My one consolation was Abuser attacking in front of their

brother and sister. They finally got to witness how aggressive they could be. In this case, we were sitting next to each other, Abuser with a wooden framed picture of the kids in their hand. Without warning, with both hands, they bodily swung it towards my face. I saw it coming and knew there was nothing I could do in time to stop it.

When I uncurled from a defensive position and opened my eyes, Abuser had vanished, their sister was crying and their brother insisted on driving me to hospital. The medical staff thought he had done it so I said I had done it to myself. A dozen stitches later, I went home then went to work for another night shift. Was still on a zero hours contract and couldn't afford not to go. This meant not being able to call the police until the following day and this, combined with Abuser's Oscar-winning tear-filled 'victim' performance, when it finally went to court in 2014. The jury found them not guilty. Were they completely untouchable? It really felt that way.

Back in 2013, a week after smashing my face, Abuser tried breaking in by climbing the fence and using our BBQ to smash the patio door. After three hits, I opened it before the glass gave in."

Abuser with the BBQ in hand, to force their way in. Victim restrained them until the police arrived. June 2013

"They were arrested – it was the last time our boys saw them, crying in the back of the police car. In my victim statements, I had repeatedly asked for Abuser to get help with mental health. "

2014

"After a year in both family and criminal courts, with Abuser being convicted of several Court Order breaches, two multi-agency assessments deemed us at HIGH RISK, of serious harm or death, and I was advised to move myself and our kids away from our home, while Abuser was held on remand at HMP Peterborough. This idea was really hard and I resisted. It would mean abandoning work, friends, home and school. And there were no refuges for males in the UK so we had to become homeless, to qualify for help in the chosen new area."

2015

"Despite Abuser's on-going attacks, with endless false claims against me, after another year in criminal and family courts, I was granted sole custody, with permission to change the kids names and no direct contact allowed by Abuser.

At the final family court hearing, Abuser did not attend - just emailed the judge, which he read out in court. Abuser called the judicial system corrupt, all police rapists and all social services child abusers. They also demanded a stay in proceedings for me to be psychiatrically assessed. The judge, having met me and Abuser on multiple occasions, was not impressed. He stated their email was evidence they knew when the hearing was and had chosen not to attend; stated nobody had expressed concerns regarding my mental health and proceeded with the final hearing as scheduled."

2018

"Abuser was from Latvia's second city, Daugavpils, which has a large ethnically Polish population. Their sister is high up in cultural circles there so, when the President of Poland, came to visit, Abuser got to meet him in person. It seems they had time to chat together too. Time enough for Abuser to convince him they were indeed the victim, for a strange thing then happened to my Polish email account. It got blocked.

The reason given was *'You have not used it for 2 years'*, which was ridiculous as used it most days. The demand to unblock it was to provide them with my address and other contact details.

I declined and abandoned that account."

Abuser with new husband and the then Polish President, Andrzej Duda, in 2018

2020

Email from Abuser: 10th January 2020, 11.24

I was a nice amazing person everybody loved and still loves...You damaged kids psychological health by kidnapping them from the loving mother. On 6th of march 2013 I took them to school (although you wrote that you did) and kissed the happy, calm children. If I knew that the monster is going to start destroying their lives after this- I would take them and run but who could predict that the father can hate his own sons as much as you do. Paul and Alan can call me any time on XXXX.

Bear in mind, the family court order specifically prohibits all direct contact between Abuser and the children, which they know but want to ignore – in line with their previously stated view that they are above the law and the multiple court order breaches affirming their view of this. Why they are so fixated on who took the children to school on 6th March is interesting, not least because, according to Victim, neither of them did.

"We lived across the road from the school, the grounds literally 100 yards from our front door. Both Abuser and I stood in the doorway to ensure they crossed the road safely and waved them goodbye."

I can only assume, Abuser is attempting to claim they took them to give self-assurance. Affirm a need to believe, in their own mind, they were a kind, loving, caring parent - unfairly torn from their children, for no good reason. What ever they tell themself and any others who will listen, the evidence in no way supports this view.

Abuser, as many abusers, committed further breaches of the indefinite Restraining Order. To this day, there remains a UK wide warrant for their arrest."

"Even now, in 2025, they email abuse - claiming they are innocent and were set up, by me with and corrupt officials. Abuser's email after their birthday in 2020, simply said this:

'You shits forgot my birthday'

Shits? Nothing about love for the boys or asking how they are, just calling us all shits. Bear in mind Abuser hasn't wished them happy birthday, happy Christmas or happy anything for the last 10 years. Hasn't given any financial support either - despite stealing the property we bought for the kids as an inheritance. And on my birthday they emailed:

'I have a brilliant memory and do remember your birthday yet cannot wish anything nice to the monster who ruined my sons lives.'

"In reality, I saved our sons' lives. Mine too."

Final Words

"Abuser was very open about wanting me dead – even in front of the kids, which terrified them more than I realised. When we escaped I had almost died several times, so exhausted my eyes would stop seeing, at 70mph. Murder by deliberate sleep deprivation. Kicking the bedroom door open shouting 'get up you lazy bastard', 2 hours after getting home from a night shift. Their goodbye wishes before I started a shift would be: *'I want you to crash and die.'*

Everything always was and always will be about the narcissist's needs, not yours. If they claim otherwise, regardless of gender, they are lying to get something for them. Never forget that."

Chapter A

Johnny Depp

Abuser or Victim?

Amber Heard claimed Johnny was a wife beater who made her fear for her life. Johnny claimed he was not the abuser but the victim. To try and get to the truth, I am going to focus on the psychology of an abuser and a victim as best I can.

These are my views, not a diagnosis of Johnny or Amber, based on available evidence, my personal experience of abusers and victims, and professional training in psychotherapy. Please note this was written before the outcomes of the related British and American court trials.

General Abuser Psychology

Abusers are takers

Weak inside: Psychopaths, sociopaths and those with narcissistic personality disorders all have a big thing in common: zero empathy. Such people feel no remorse or sorrow for any suffering of others. They are happy to give their victims horror and hurt, focused on 'owning' them, as a means to their ends. These ends involve some kind of ego gain: financial, social status, power, admiration from others. Why do they need this? Because they have what is termed a 'fragile ego' - so weak they can't stand criticism or being exposed.

If 'attacked' by a question, instead of answering it, they throw a question back at the questioner; belittle the question or shout and rage, with tears on tap regardless of gender - anything to avoid answering the actual question as long as possible. If there is someone else they can think to blame, they will. Their ego is too weak to accept criticism or admit wrong doing, even to themselves, for admission would mean acknowledging their lies and how terrible they were.

This weak ego usually stems from infancy, prior to 6-months of age, when they felt so much stress their developing brain was unable to cope with the levels of cortisol, stress hormone, flooding through it - permanently damaging their brain's ability to handle stress. In adulthood they seek deflections, such as praise and admiration, to stroke their pained inner child but it doesn't fix it. Lacking empathy they have no qualms about hurting others, caring only about getting more stroking for their inner child.

Unable to face the reality of their abusive ways, including evidence they have wronged, they project their pain onto others. With all the anger, rage, loneliness and abandonment from their infancy that has never gone away such projection is the only mechanism they have for coping. As this projection only lets off steam but fails to deal with the actual issues, nothing improves.

Abuse includes belittling, controlling, raging, manipulation, wild accusations (the more dramatic the better), violence and blame; often twisting a story around some true moment, used as the root for the lies they weave.

General Victim Psychology

Victims are Givers

Strong inside: patient, love for others above love for self (co-dependent), a sense of proving self-worth by supporting and looking after others, even if this means taking damage in the process. Defence mechanisms include escape (alcohol, drugs, location) until ready to face their abuser again and try again to go forward - until the next abuse starts and the whole process repeats.

This psychology can stem from 6-months of age onwards. Although the brain has developed good cortisol stress handling, some later event(s) make the person doubt their self-worth, often giving them a subconscious lifescript of 'unlovable' or 'unworthy', which leaves them losing love for themselves and focusing on feeling loved by giving it to others.

If you answer yes to one or more of these questions, you may be experiencing domestic abuse:

Does your partner constantly belittle or humiliate you, or regularly criticise or insult you?

Has your partner ever hurt or threatened you or your children?

Has your partner ever forced you to do something that you really did not want to do?

Has your partner ever tried to prevent your leaving the house?

Has your partner prevented you or made it hard for you to continue or start studying, or from going to work?

Copyright: *Women's Aid, Survivors Handbook, Am I in an Abusive Relationship?*, used with thanks.

As a victim of domestic violence myself, I agree with these indicators. Let's look at two of them.

'Does your partner constantly belittle or humiliate you, or regularly criticise or insult you?'

and

'Has your partner ever hurt or threatened you or your children?'

Johnny and Amber often recorded each other during their marriage. Below is a transcript and link to part of one such recording. According to the Daily Mail on 20th July 2020, this is from a secret recording Johnny made of him with Amber and was released by his legal team during the 2020 High-Court trial.

This is not the full recording, just an extract and we join them about 30 minutes in. Many longer audio clips of this, including what came before and after can be found on Youtube, such as *Amber Heard Taunts Johnny Depp - another audio leaked!*

Here I have focused on a section found particularly interesting. When you listen to the tone and intonations in the recording, bear in mind these questions:

A) Any fear in anyone's voice?

B) Any aggression in anyone's voice?

C) Anyone raising their voice?

D) Anyone admitting to being violent and seeming to think that is OK?

E) Anyone belittling?

F) Anyone trying to twist/manipulate events?

Widely available in the public domain, this extract has been posted on Victim's Youtube Channel for review purposes, with stills from Instagram. Any errors in the transcript are entirely unintentional. The copyright holders of the original files are unknown but used with thanks.

https://www.youtube.com/watch?v=76wfaiB7zpA

AMBER	...if you have something you're holding onto about Travis, fucking go. Fucking... Go fuck. You know? Go do it. Go run away together. I don't know what you're fucking holding onto. But you have created that. I have no part of that. I don't know what you fucking latched onto in your brain, what stray hairs have fucking co-mingled and tangled in your brain to make you think you've really figured something out but this is not unusual for you.

	It's like almost every fight I can pretty much guarantee you'll find something that you can like...
JOHNNY	Let's, let's ask Travis tonight.
AMBER	Yes, why don't we invite Travis, into... into our fucked up, broken assed, 3-fucking wheeled, truck of a marriage? Why don't we crash it straight into the wall because no-one knows us better than fucking Travis.
JOHNNY	You're just afraid that the truth will come out.
AMBER	What truth?
JOHNNY	That you lied.
AMBER	What are you fucking talking about? I didn't fucking even have a fucking thing to lie about. What are you fucking talking? Every fucking fight there's a new thing that you convince yourself that's a lie...
JOHNNY	No. I said to you: "Amber, tell Travis what you just did."
AMBER	(scoffs and laughs)
JOHNNY	That you just fucking...that you punched me in the fucking jaw. That you fucking kicked... Did you? Did you? And you wouldn't say a fucking... You said: "I don't know what you're talking about... It never fucking.... It never fucking happened."
AMBER	I see the light. I see the light. You really should run with this. In fact maybe you and Travis can like... Go and like, you know, do a tell all about... You know, an investigate study.
JOHNNY	Stop. Stop with the attitude. Right? Stop with the attitude. Getting all bunched
AMBER	What ever you think happened with Travis. Every conversation you...
JOHNNY	Listen. I was not high. You lied.
AMBER	I am not going to...
JOHNNY	You lied your ass off.
AMBER	You're fucking full of shit. What lie?
JOHNNY	You lied your ass off.
AMBER	When? What conversation did I have with Travis? On this big, big investigative study you've done. I'm not sitting here fighting with you about the...

JOHNNY	No, I was in a situation with you
AMBER	About the fight that we had last night.
JOHNNY	After you fucking got physically violent with me, I texted Travis and said 'Come up here' because I didn't want anything to happen.
AMBER	No....
JOHNNY	He's coming to what? Save me?
AMBER	No. Go ahead. Continue. You, you, you... Travis to the rescue.
JOHNNY	No. That was the last one. You can go, er... Go. That was the last insult.
AMBER	You, you call me a liar and yet, yet... Yet.
JOHNNY	I watched you lie.
AMBER	You called me a liar
JOHNNY	I watched you lie. I heard it. I was right there.
AMBER	There's no...What? You still haven't told me what lie it is.
JOHNNY	We talked...
AMBER	Yet every single fucking time. You know you do this every single fucking time.
JOHNNY	We'll talk to Travis. We'll talk to Travis.
AMBER	I'm not fucking talking to nobody. Fuck that. You go fucking jerk... Go jerk him off. I don't care. I really couldn't care less. It's you. Every single time you latch onto some sort of thing when I already told you, I don't know what you're fucking talking about. You don't even know what you're talking about. You still haven't even told me what it is. You run with it. You...
JOHNNY	I have told you what it is.
AMBER	No you haven't.
JOHNNY	I said to Travis. No. I said to you: "Hey, tell Travis what just happened. You..."
AMBER	You told me to do it. You told me to. You said: "Go do that."
JOHNNY	I said, no, tell him what just happened.
AMBER	And I lied.
JOHNNY	And that you punched me in the fucking thing, in the face.

176

AMBER	...you reckon...you figured it all out...
JOHNNY	And you said... "Oh, fuck it. No I didn't. What the fuck are you talking about?" And I watched you lie and then I...
AMBER	I didn't punch you. I didn't punch you, by the way. You.
JOHNNY	You punched me.
AMBER	I'm sorry that I didn't, er, hit you across the face in a proper slap but I was hitting you. It was not punching you. Babe, you're not punched.
JOHNNY	Don't tell me what it feels like to be punched.
AMBER	You know, you've been in a lot of fights. I know it's been a long time. I know...
JOHNNY	No, when you fucking have a closed fist.
AMBER	You didn't get punched. You're not hit. I'm sorry I hit you like this, but I did not punch you. I did not fucking deck you. I fucking was hitting you.
JOHNNY	You...
AMBER	I don't know what the motion of my actual hand was but you're fine. I did not hurt you. I did not punch you. I was hitting you.
JOHNNY	How are your toes?
AMBER	How? What am I supposed to do? Do this?
JOHNNY	How are your toes?
AMBER	I'm not sitting here bitching about it, am I? You are. That's the difference between me and you.
JOHNNY	How are your poor toes?
AMBER	You're a fucking baby.
JOHNNY	Because you start physical fights.
AMBER	You are such a baby. Shut the fuck up.
JOHNNY	Because you start physical fights.
AMBER	I did start a physical fight.
JOHNNY	Yeah, you did so I had to get the fuck out of there.
AMBER	Yes, you did. So you did the right thing. The big thing. The.. You know what? You're admirable. Every single time, what's you're excuse. If there's not a physical

177

fight then what's the excuse then? You're still being admirable, right? Running away. And you could stay here and call me names. But you don't stay here and call me names, what do you do? "That's the last insult." You're a baby. You're a hypocrite. You don't do anything that you actually do. You expect from people...

James Corden Show

Amber maintains she is the victim of a wife-beater and, on 15th December 2015 there was allegedly a very major attack by Johnny.

"I had bruised ribs, bruises all over my body, bruises on my forearms from trying to defend the blows. I had two black eyes. I had a broken nose. I had a broken lip. I had bruises primarily. The really bad ones were in my hairline, in my scalp, my chin ---

There were chunks of hair missing, there was pus in those wounds, in my hairline, dark red bruises specifically, like, purple/red on my temples and in my chin. The inside of my upper lip was cut."

Testimony by Amber Heard – Page 1912, Day 12, British High Court hearing, computer-aided transcript by Marten Walsh Cherer Limited, used for reference with thanks.

Let's say Amber's claims are true, that she was heavily battered and bruised from a massive attack by Johnny, what other evidence would there be to affirm this the following day? Personally, I would expect this:

1) Stiffness of walking and movement in general. If you get beaten up to such an extent it will be painful to move about, to gesticulate, even to smile and talk. A broken, even 'just' fractured nose would surely be visibly swollen.

2) Psychological damage. You would be emotional, downcast, sullen, upset, less perky than usual, withdrawn.

Watch Amber's appearance on the James Corden show, the day after this alleged massive attack, to judge for yourself:

Youtube Channel: The Late Late Show with James Corden

Video: *"Amber Heard Has a Ballet Claw"*

Posted: 17th December 2015.

178

Other Background Information

In the UK the Telegraph reported that Amber's sister, Whitney, was beaten up by Amber and filmed with physical injuries.

Youtube Channel: The Telegraph

Video: *Video shows 'Amber Heard beat up her sister Whitney', High Court told*

Posted: 24th July 2020

According to Maria Puente, on September 14th 2009, Amber was arrested for physically assaulting her partner, Tasya van Ree, though no charges were pressed.

Full article: *Amber Heard arrested in 2009 on charge of hitting girlfriend*

Published by: USA Today, June 2016

Written by: Maria Puente.

Reportedly, at the behest of Amber Heard, private investigator Paul Barresi was hired to 'dig up dirt' on Johnny Depp. After some 100 interviews, on people who knew/worked with Johnny over a 30 year period, not a bad word was said about him, though quite a lot of bad words were said about Amber. Paul's 'employment' was terminated and these findings were not presented to the High Court.

Full article: *Amber Heard hired P.I. to dig up dirt on Johnny Depp, but 'fixer' spoke to 100 people who all 'couldn't say enough about his generosity and tender heart' - but some had harsh words for actress*

Published by: the Daily Mail, 1st April 2020,

Written by: Chris White

UK Trial Media Reports

The following newspaper extracts are used for review purposes, with thanks to the respective copyright holders:

Owen Boycott and Caroline Davies, **The Guardian**, 3rd November 2020 quote:

Lisa King from Refuge: *"...every survivor of domestic abuse should be listened to. No survivor should ever have her voice silenced"* and

Harriet Wistrich, founder of the Centre for Women's Justice: *"...a really helpful judgement and will serve as a warning to men who think they can silence those who speak out about their abuse."*

and

"Nicki Norman, acting chief executive at Women's Aid: *"...Everyone who has experienced domestic abuse deserves to be listened to and believed..."*

David Brown, **the Saturday Times**, on 7th November wrote: Harriet Wistrich, founder of the Centre for Women's Justice, led the calls for Depp to be dropped after the judgement: *"It sends out a really bad message to allow him to continue to have a platform."*

Chris Pollard, **the Sun**, on 7th November wrote: TOXIC wife beater Johnny Depp will never work in Hollywood again following his axing from Fantastic Beasts, says a top lawyer.

Meanwhile, Jenny Afia, a solicitor at Schillings who represented him, was quoted in the Guardian article, on 3rd November, as saying: *"This decision is as perverse as it is bewildering."*

On Johnny Depp's Instagram page, on 6th November 2020, he wrote: *"...Firstly, I'd like to thank everybody who has gifted me their support and loyalty. I have been humbled and moved by your many messages of love... The surreal judgement of the court in the UK. Will not change my fight to tell the truth and I confirm that I plan to appeal...."*

While Amber's supporters claim she is now being trolled and subjected to further abuse, personally, I see it as the other way round. And the majority of the public following these events seem to agree it is actually Johnny who is the real victim, being relentlessly further abused. Why would millions of people support him if there was any evidence he was a wife beater? I certainly wouldn't.

When Johnny announced he had been asked to resign from the Fantastic Beasts films because of the court judgement against him, his following didn't diminish. Instead it grew even stronger. His Instagram followers have been increasing at the rate of 100,000 a day and now exceed 8.5 million, of which I am one. A petition to Warner Brothers to get him re-instated has got over a million signatures - still climbing, while a petition to get Amber removed from Aquaman 2 also has a million signatures - still climbing.

What Happened Next?

In 2022 a jury trial in the USA gave a polar opposite verdict. Johnny was awarded the maximum punitive damages that Virginia State law allowed: $350,000. Amber was found guilty of defamation on all three counts, including with malicious intent.

Having followed the cases and their behaviours, I fully support the US verdict and feel ashamed regarding the British one.

Like I said, this is not a diagnosis. In my personal view, as a survivor of domestic abuse and as a therapist, I have not seen not a shred of supporting medical, psychological, pathological or eye-witness evidence against him. In contrast, I believe I have seen abusive behaviour demonstrated by Amber, according to the indicators in Women's Aid's handbook.

While not a formal diagnosis, I have perceived a characteristic in Johnny which is often found in victims of domestic abuse: co-dependency. This characteristic involves putting someone else's happiness, especially our partner's, ahead of our own. The need to walk away from the fights that Amber admits she starts, is similar to what I used to do with my abusive wife; when it became clear she only want to rant, rage and attack, I would shut myself away - leave the house, sleep in my car or a hotel and get drunk to psychologically escape; much to the annoyance of my abuser as she had then lost her punchbag. I see this as being exactly what Johnny was doing to escape abuser Amber.

Further Viewing

This is a video of Amber testifying shortly after their marriage, with interesting comments and comparisons regarding her behaviour:

Youtube channel: The Dialogue Body Language

Video: *Amber Heard -Unicorns and Rainbows- Nothing to See here Boys! Body Language*

Posted: 21st April 2019

Chapter B

John's Story

Colleagues began to see my injuries

"In 1997 met my ex wife for the first time, 9 years younger than me - very petite, 4ft 10" tall and very attractive. I have to say I did like her. I had just joined GMP as a Police Officer after 5 years as a special constable - loved my job, it was my dream to become an officer.

To summarise the next 13 years as best I can, she systematically abused me both physically and mentally; isolated me from my family and friends. Made me feel like it was my fault. Jealousy and accusations of affairs - she used coercive control very effectively. I've been spat at, stabbed with a fork, hit over the head with a blunt object, kicked in the groin, had jewellery ripped from my neck and clothes ripped from my back. Been bruised badly on my arms and torso, bitten, black eyes.

I don't know how or why I put up with it but we did have 3 beautiful children, which she threatened to take from me and to make lose my job and house. She drank to excess; hated our neighbours; caused problems with women at school with her snide comments. Colleagues began to see my injuries. Her own mother and step father began to see them too but I was so isolated after falling out with my family because of her attitude.

I got the highest commendation for bravery from the Chief Constable, made off duty arrests of dangerous criminals wanted for 6 months and letters of appreciation from members of the public, including two heart attack victims I gave first aid as they both survived. Yet, when I disclosed I was suffering DV to my line manager in 2009 no positive action was taken.

I informed my ex of this and her response was to try and commit suicide. Late 2009 she attacked me again and admitted it in court - I suffered bruises, spat in my face and 3 kicks to the groin; witnessed in part by our little girl. I had no choice but to protect myself from her drunken attack and slapped her hard across the face - this led to my arrest.

I informed officers of my historical abuse but this was ignored. Those who had witnessed my injuries were ignored and after a 3 day trial I was convicted of common assault. I lost my job because of the conviction. She refused me access to our 3 kids, took my home and most of my pension.

I now have reports from a DV expert and self defence expert who state I'm innocent, and photographs of historical injuries all never seen by a court but the Criminal Case Review Commission refused to allow me an appeal. Nearly ten years later I still protest my innocence and want an appeal to bring my ex, the real perpetrator, to justice. And I had to do all this, despite being a well-respected police officer."

Chapter C
The Duluth Model

Originating in the 1980's in Duluth, Minnesota, this is a Stone-Age domestic violence model that focuses only on physical violence and male perpetrators. It has no place in a modern society claiming to look at all elements of domestic violence and consider all perpetrators, regardless of gender - yet the Duluth model is, in practice, how the vast majority of the UK family court and (in)justice system operates.

Duluth Model

- Prioritizes the voices and experiences of women who experience battering in the creation of those policies and procedures.
- Believes that battering is a pattern of actions used to intentionally control or dominate an intimate partner and actively works to change societal conditions that support men's use of tactics of power and control over women.

This factually incorrect model is, pretty much single-handedly, responsible for supporting the millions of injustices against male victims and their children. By automatically and very incorrectly assuming the female is always the victim, female abusers are not just given support but empowered to be more abusive. As Abuser said, *"They believe women"*:

This model has become so ingrained in British society and media, especially by Channel 4 News, and so completely followed that many male victims are left so abandoned they feel their only option is to take the verbal/psychological abuse or take their own lives. Many of those who dare ask for help come away worse – discovering the system is so systemically against them, as males, that often they are labelled the abuser.

This is not only an unfair and injust position, it is one with no basis in reality or fact.

Most DV Victims are Male?

While the independent British Crime Study results find the abuse ratio is far closer to 50-50. Professor Kevan, a female, has gone further and studied the topic in a way that allows people to share their experiences more openly – her findings are that most victims of domestic violence are male, not female.

Youtube Channel: Justice for Men & Boys, & the women who love them

Video: *7 June 2020:* Prof Nicola Graham-Kevan's keynote speech, "Coercive Control and Domestic Violence"

Other Cases & Conclusions

Below are some other victim overviews, used with kind permission. The full versions can be found on the Mankind Initiative website:

https://www.mankind.org.uk/

Fiona's Story:

Fiona was very worried about her son Greg being abused by his wife, who does not allow him to work any more because she says he would spend all day looking at other women. He appears with bruises, is banned from a mobile and was locked out the house with the children, while his wife phoned the police lying he is abusive and hits the children. Though repeatedly seriously injured by her, Greg remained afraid to leave for fear of the children's safety...

Matthew's story:

A month after our first baby was born, she started arguing on the way home, stating that I had belittled her in front of her friends. She was becoming very aggressive. At home, she began shouting and smashed a mirror over my head. The next morning she was as if nothing had happened. A few weeks later, working 60 hours a week and exhausted from night feeds, I turned down an extra shift – she started arguing, saying she wanted new clothes. Every time I tried to talk she would shout over the top of me and smashed a glass door, throwing the pieces at me. I escaped. The next morning, I returned home to her crying, saying that she was sorry and it would never happen again.

She started going out a lot more, leaving me at home with our child and becoming aggressive again. She was using cocaine and cheating - which she blamed on me but I still loved her and was desperate to make it work. One night she attacked me and I ran to phone the police and she phoned them too. We were both arrested then told no further action would be taken, even though I had marks on me and she didn't.

I was accused of cheating. She jumped on me, biting and scratching me all over my face. I told the kids to run to their bedrooms but they wouldn't leave me...

184

Jamie's Story:

The first three months of our marriage were excellent, then I was promoted and she became very insecure - resenting my promotion so much and she wanted me to give up the £50k salary and take a job as a bin man. I refused and she hit me. I had never been hit in a relationship before and it shocked me.

She apologised - then I would get hit across the face, shoes or plates thrown at me. It became the routine. I would come back from work, have something to eat, we would argue about my job and I would get hit. One night I told her that I did not love her any more because of her violence – she began punching and kicking me then drove off in a rage...

Sam's story:

I was with my wife for six years and did everything I could for her but soon learnt nothing would ever be enough. Emotional abuse started first – only allowed to go out alone to work and even then she would phone constantly. I tried to leave but she emotionally blackmailed me by overdosing on tablets; which I later found she spat out under the bed. She also threatened to hurt any future girlfriends so badly I wouldn't want to be with them.

After two years, thinking things could get better, I proposed - the biggest mistake of my life and things went downhill. I don't know why but she ran into the house, grabbed a knife and attack me. She grabbed my testicles and twisted them hard - excruciatingly painful. The second time she attacked, she followed me around the house punching me in the head, hitting me with a pint glass, knocked me to the floor and repeatedly dropped her knee on to my head...

Graham's Story:

Graham was married to his wife for 10 years before he felt strong enough to leave. During their marriage his wife was violent to both him and their son - she had a drink problem, which made the violence worse and would use this as an excuse after every attack, promising to change.

Graham even tried to commit suicide twice throughout their marriage because he did not know where to go for help. During her final attack, he was stabbed in the head by his wife... He was kept from seeing his son for 2 years but was eventually granted sole custody...

Sebastian's story:

Sebastian is 6ft, his 5ft 3inch partner became violent after becoming pregnant. After months of abuse, he could take no more and decided to leave but she threatened that if he left he would never see his son again. Her abuse increased: black eyes, spat at and a chair thrown with such force it shattered on him. He is not allowed to go to bed before her –if he does she comes in and turns all the lights on and begins shouting to prevent him from getting to sleep...

There are several commonalities here. The first is the focus on physical abuse, with none of the victims escaping on the grounds of emotional or psychological abuse, which requires other forms of evidence to be believed. The second is the pattern of escalation of abuse, with the abusers demonstrating regard only for themselves. The third is the lack of support or victim attempts to get support for anything except major and blatant physical abuse. A lot of people, especially males, find it not just too embarrassing to tell others they are raged at but that no-one will believe them or care. Even with evidence of physical abuse, police declined to take action against Sebastian's partner. As for Graham, just how many lies did his wife tell to stop him seeing his son for two years? Would the courts ever do that to a mother stabbed by her husband? Men are, all too often, simply expected to take it.

As for suicides, how many male suicides are due to the sense of helplessness in abusive relationships because they are simply and systemically not taken seriously? This was Victim's experience too, until her was able to evidence the abuse by recording his wife 24/7, including on camera.

Conclusions

According to Women's Aid: *'In the vast majority of cases it* (domestic abuse) *is experienced by women and is perpetrated by men'.*

This disputed statement follows the Duluth model, itself disputed. What is not disputed is almost all of those prosecuted for domestic abuse in the UK (some 92%) are male, yet at least a third of victims are male (1,300,000 female, 695,000 male – British Crime Survey, 2018) so why the imbalance?

Males are often too ashamed to admit suffering coercive, psychological, physical and emotional abuse; made to feel it is irrelevant, normal or simply get laughed at and told to 'man up'. It seems male victims so rarely even get to court they don't even count in many of the statistics.

In 2015, I sent Freedom of Information Requests to police forces throughout the UK - which revealed police were up to eight times more likely to prosecute males accused of abuse than females accused of abuse. Systemic gender bias? Should this be surprising considering the stance by organisations like Women's Aid and national media. Just look at the number of people who ran to stomp on Johnny Depp when Amber Heard accused him of abuse. In 2011, Kier Starmer, then DPP, gave a long speech about domestic violence and not once, not one single time, did he mention male victims. It was entirely focused on females. In 2015, I wrote to Alison Saunders, the new DPP, and asked her about systemic gender bias against male victims. Who replied? It wasn't Alison Saunders, it was a representative from the department for *Violence against Women and Girls* – no mention of violence against men or even boys.

So it is with the support of such gender bias, abuser Abuser felt carte blanch to do what ever she wanted. In her own words:

Transcript: 3rd March 2013, 1.25pm -
https://www.youtube.com/watch?v=0uNJOtpexm8

ABUSER	I know how the system works, they believe women.

For non-physical, less visible yet potentially more damaging categories of abuse we have psychological, emotional, controlling, coercive, financial *(I'll take the house)* and threatening *(I'll take the kids)*. Even for the physical, if a female is attacking a male we have been Carry-On-film brainwashed into smiling as she shouts *(He's really getting an ear bashing)* or starts hitting *(She's really letting him have it)*.

The reality, as any victim will tell you if not too ashamed to admit it, is horrifying. If a male victim goes to the authorities for help he often ends up labelled the abuser. All an abusive female has to do is sob crocodile tears, crying she is the poor little victim and, even when there is evidence against her, she is most likely to be believed - which is exactly what Abuser states above. Knowing this, female abusers don't just feel empowered to do what ever they want they are empowered to. They have become, quite literally, state supported and untouchable abusers.

Believe males are able to defend themselves if a female gets too physical? On a desert island that may well be the case but in our 'civilised' society this is mostly nonsense - the second a male victim tries to even push back his female abuser can have him arrested and charged - even though it was just self-defence against her attacks.

Every victim has a breaking point and, having looked into this topic for some years now, I wonder how many acts of violence, logged as male-perpetrated domestic abuse, are actually eruptions of pent up fury after years of relentless abuse by their female partner. Sally Challen was released from prison, under appeal in 2019, after killing her abusive husband with a hammer during such an explosion. Justifiable homicide is the label that has been given and I am on her side yet where is the balance? What about those males imprisoned for doing the same, yet with no chance of appeal or any such sympathy? No-one can condone violence but, when a system is so twisted it fails to protect true victims, it is only human when the victim reaches breaking point and fights back.

"I never hit women.", states Victim, **"The one time I hit Abuser was after a four-hour verbal, psychological and then physical assault, including them pouring a tin of paint over me and my home office. As I was trying to save my drowning cameras, they stood in the doorway and threatened to do worse. I couldn't take worse. I snapped.**

If Abuser had got help with their personality disorder or at least been forced to curb their aggressions, rather than social service's carte blanch ticket to abuse with impunity, maybe they wouldn't have become the monster they did. Our children would still have both parents and we wouldn't have had to move away to escape. Instead they were made to feel untouchable, convinced they were above the law and could lie their way through anything they did, no matter how awful. For years they did just that."

Find the audio and video recordings on **Youtube**

@abusedmen7480

https://www.youtube.com/@abusedmen7480

Domestic Violence – *escaping murder*

Copyright © 1999-2025 BR Stone

Front cover picture is an actual CCTV image from Victim's arrest in 2008.

This edit: 15th November 2025

This book is based on fact. *Logs, transcripts and situations are real. Only names and locations have been changed to protect identities.*

The chapter on Johnny Depp expresses my personal views based on available evidence, experience of abuse and professional training in psychotherapy. Worth noting is the UK judge-led court totally went against him, while the US jury court did the exact opposite.

I am a qualified therapist, working in private practice and a full member (MBACP) of the British Association of Counsellors and Psychotherapists.

Other books by BR Stone

After Abuse – *your recovery*

Identify the Abuser – *narcissists uncovered*

Parenting Infant Minds – *brain growth matters*

Depression – *bye bye*

Anxiety – *12-step help*

Anxiety & Addictions – *break the cycle*

therapybrad.co.uk

Printed in Dunstable, United Kingdom